When someone from your organization
approaches an existing customer, or potential prospect —
what does your value proposition look like to them?

This?

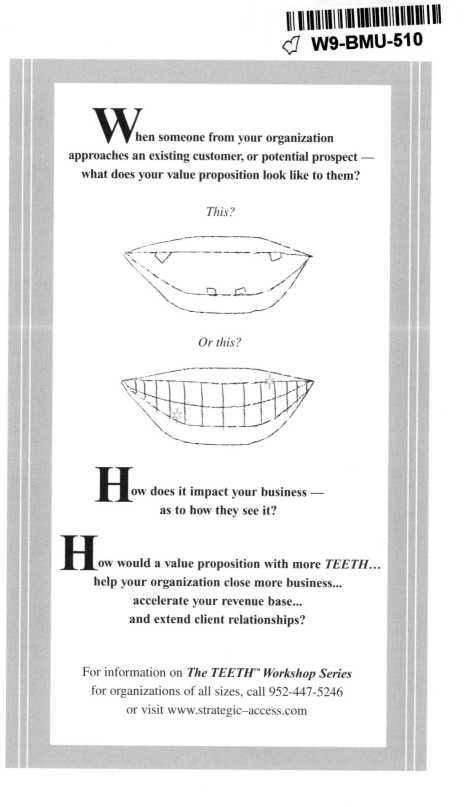

Or this?

How does it impact your business —
as to how they see it?

How would a value proposition with more *TEETH...*
help your organization close more business...
accelerate your revenue base...
and extend client relationships?

For information on *The TEETH™ Workshop Series*
for organizations of all sizes, call 952-447-5246
or visit www.strategic–access.com

If You Are Looking for a Proven Keynote Speaker Who Delivers — for Your Next Annual or Quarterly Meeting or Convention — Read This First...

"We have had the pleasure of working with **'the best of the best' speakers and trainers**... Dr. Ken Blanchard, co-author of *The One Minute Manager*, Dr. Stephen Covey, author of *The Seven Habits of Highly Effective People,* Tom Peters, author of *In Search of Excellence*, and several other of the most notable speakers in the country. These speakers and internationally acclaimed authors are some of the best speakers in the business, however, Michael brought our audience alive with insights and ideas that will change the way they approach their business forever.

His general session keynote at our Annual Convention in Las Vegas was our **all-time highest rated keynote** — and his general session keynote address in Dallas was **rated the highest of all keynotes ever**, since the inception of The ASI! Show.

The way in which he engaged and involved an audience of thousands was incredible and effective. He is a fabulous speaker... one that we trust to deliver content that is **on-point, relevant**, and **timely** with the current market conditions, and one that we trust to deliver strong value for our members.

We highly recommend Michael, his organization, and program offerings for any organization considering them, and we look forward to working with him again on future national programs."

—**Natalie Pyatt Townes,**
Director of Education & Training
The ASI! Show (The Advertising Specialties Institute of America)

Additional Praise for This Material

"Before embracing the principles of *TEETH*, we had solid solutions and we were able to effectively describe 'what' our solutions did in terms of features and functions. With *TEETH*, we can now describe to executives the 'so what' of our value propositions in terms of financial impact. By changing our focus from 'what' to 'so what', *TEETH* not only improved our ability to sell our current solutions, it has also helped us keep our new product development focused on what is really important to our customers. By having value propositions with *TEETH*, we are now selling business solutions versus technical solutions, and we are selling more effectively to the real decision makers."

—Mike Meyer,
Chief Executive Officer
LogicaCMG Americas

"I think *TEETH* is a very common-sense, practical, and down-to-earth look at value propositions, and what they mean to clients — and can do for organizations. I believe value propositions have implications inside an organization also — not just to clients. Without an in-depth understanding of a company's value proposition, its employees won't do the right things, at the right time, for the right reasons."

—John Murray,
President & Chief Executive Officer
PLATO Learning, Inc.

"Michael Boylan's new book *TEETH* is an outstanding handbook for driving sales results. It provides a proven framework for developing and delivering high value sales messages to executive level decision makers."

—Ken Gitlin,
Executive Director
Robert Half International Inc.

"*TEETH* is one of those rare business books that has a simple, but powerful and to the point message. When I got to the end I said to myself, 'the message was so clear, compelling, and obvious — why didn't I think of that?'"

—Steve Prentiss,
Senior Vice President
ADP Brokerage Services Group

"Better and more frequent access/exposure to 'C' level executives and shortened sales cycles. What Fortune 500 sales organization would not want to improve in these two areas? This material helps the senior management and the sales, marketing, and delivery organizations to articulate the core results of what their products, services, and solutions really deliver — the true value of their offerings, which is so needed nowadays, because most cannot do it very well. *TEETH* is a must read for everyone who considers him/herself serious about selling, and growing market share."

—Richard Carbone,
Vice President, Sales Operations,
North American Sales & Service
Unisys Corporation

TEETH

MICHAEL A. BOYLAN

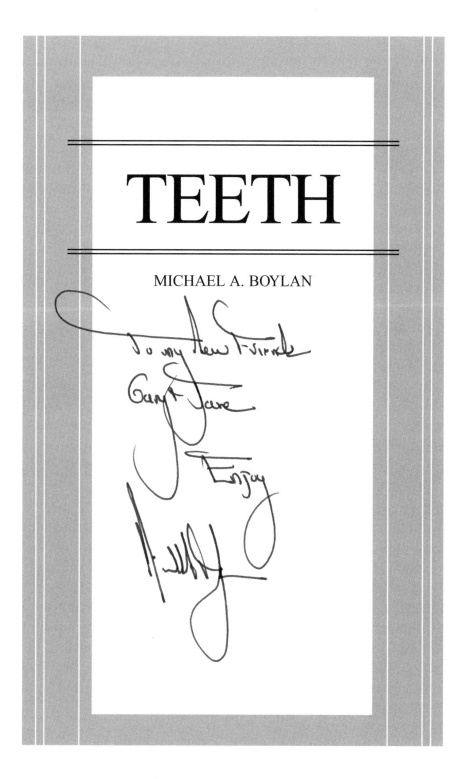

Other books by MICHAEL A. BOYLAN

The Power To Get In®
A Step-By-Step System To Get In Anyone's Door

═══════════════════

TEETH
DOES YOUR VALUE PROPOSITION HAVE ANY?

A Field-Proven Framework To
Crystallize, Condense, & Calibrate Your Message
So You Close More Business

By Michael A. Boylan

Copyright © 2004 by Michael A. Boylan
All rights reserved.
Printed in the United States of America.
Published by Strategic Press International™
First Edition — Hardcover
2 3 4 5 6 7 8 9 10
Library of Congress Cataloging-in-Publication Data
LCCN# 2002090195

ISBN 0-9717421-0-3 (hardcover)

To order, please call:
Strategic Press International™
952-447-5246

TEETH

DOES YOUR VALUE PROPOSITION HAVE ANY?

A FIELD-PROVEN FRAMEWORK TO
CRYSTALLIZE, CONDENSE, & CALIBRATE YOUR MESSAGE
SO YOU CLOSE MORE BUSINESS

MICHAEL A. BOYLAN

STRATEGIC PRESS INTERNATIONAL™

MINNEAPOLIS, MINNESOTA

TEETH

DOES YOUR VALUE PROPOSITION HAVE ANY?

A FIELD-PROVEN FRAMEWORK TO
CRYSTALLIZE, CONDENSE, & CALIBRATE YOUR MESSAGE
SO YOU CLOSE MORE BUSINESS

TEETH™ is Book One in the *TEETH*™ Series by

MICHAEL A. BOYLAN

STRATEGIC PRESS INTERNATIONAL™

MINNEAPOLIS, MINNESOTA

(952) 447-5246

TABLE OF CONTENTS

A Message Relevant For The Times

If you're wondering if this book will answer all of your questions, so you can create for your organization, a brand new or refined, crystal clear value proposition, customized around the specifics of your products, service lines and solution offerings—calibrated to the target companies and levels of access to whom you desire more exposure, that's a pretty tall order. However, what this book will do is provide a proven framework for how to begin down that path.

This path can be complex—a mega brain-teaser, causing you, your senior leadership and your sales/business development organization to engage in some intense debates about *what*, *how*, and *to whom* you should be focusing and calibrating your message and value propositions. And then of course, what *they* should communicate.

TEETH™ is the beginning piece of an ongoing program offering for organizations, helping the executive leadership teams enhance their own business health.

Our senior client executives can assist the executive leadership teams by shaping, crystallizing, and properly calibrating your initial *Corporate* value proposition. Then, perhaps shaping additional value propositions around each business unit's or division's specific offerings—which can lead to additional value propositions focused around specific product, service, or solution oriented offerings.

The fact of the matter is, ***value propositions are never—and can never remain static.*** Why? *Because business is never static.* Organizations continue to expand product, service, and solution offerings in response to trends, mergers and acquisitions, customer desires, or pure speculation.

Therefore, *a value proposition must be kept up to date—relevant and current* to your suite of offerings, and to the target markets and vertical sectors you serve.

The point is—this book is not the *be all—end all*—then after you've read it—boom— *your value propositions are fixed.*

To do it right, and to maximize the value and revenue return good ones can bring, we invite you to look into the programs we offer organizations serious about growing their business—and you will realize the tremendous power and stature that can be gained through a crystal clear, properly calibrated value proposition.

We have assisted several Fortune 1000 multi-nationals, mid-sized and smaller organizations in various vertical sectors, public and private—craft articulate, condensed and calibrated value propositions that resonate with the desired audiences to whom our clients want more access and exposure.

This arena of expertise should not be taken lightly, since it almost always strikes at the *core* of what you and your organization are trying to accomplish.

Some firms engage us initially to train their sales, business developers, and senior executives on *The Circle of Leverage® System*, a repeatable methodology providing faster, more frequent, and higher levels of access to senior executive decision makers earlier on in the selling process. Hence, providing a more powerful audience in which to present their offerings, giving them the ability to close business faster. We teach and support this methodology for our clients.

As we deliver the programs, we *and* the client discover together, that more often than not, their message is not clear, there are no compelling reasons why the prospect or client *should* pay attention to them— the sales professionals are using "29" different sets of net benefits—key points of difference—and positioning statements. Everyone is singing a different song—on different keys. And then the senior management wonders why their sales cycles are stretching, and their cost of sales is on the rise! Give us a break. To us— it's very clear, and full of common sense.

How can your organization expect to be worthy of access to those key decision makers—versus those who say they can, but can't without buy-in from 10 other people inside the organization—*if you can't communicate concisely the key reasons why they should pay attention to you?* This all points to your message and value propositions.

As business becomes even more competitive in the years ahead, we suggest that this ability becomes a *mandatory skill set* and capability within your organization—period. You will win more business as a result.

Market Timeliness and Subject Matter Relevance

If the 1990's was the beginning decade of "e"— e-business, e-commerce, web this and web that, then beginning with this book, the first decade of the 2000's may become known as *The Decade of the Message.*

With the economic cool-down of 2001, 2002, and 2003, and the genuine concern, fear, and guardedness that thousands of businesses and business professionals are feeling, we believe the executive leadership teams within each organization are looking for down to earth, principle-based, proven patterns of success to emulate for their organizations. When businesses experience difficult times, history reveals that they tend to *revert back to the basics*—meaning, a reassessment of what's important to the core success of their business, such as finding the answers to questions like:

- *What is our core business?*
- *What is it that we are really selling?*

- *Let's take a hard look at the audience(s) we're selling to.*
- *Are we selling to the right people? Is our message getting to the right people? And how do we know?*
- *And what is our message—really? Let's take a hard look at our message and value propositions. Are they correct? Do they communicate what we need to communicate to the people we're trying to reach?*

The programs based on this material help the executive leadership teams by using these methodologies to help them *reassess, crystallize and condense, calibrate and articulate their core message/value propositions* to the exact audiences to whom they desire more access and exposure, creating huge value and return on investment. In plain language—it helps them to be *clearer, more credible, more worthy, and more easily understood.* And that—helps drive top line revenues.

TEETH and The *TEETH* Workshops are designed to help business leaders genuinely *ready* to take a hard look at finding the right answers to the above questions for their organization.

—A Point of Clarification

Please note that when we refer to access—this material applies to those sales and business development professionals, senior account managers, and management responsible for growing the revenue streams from *existing customer accounts.* Meaning, they already have access inside the account with multiple contacts, but wish to expand their influence, and executive levels of access or exposure, to provide progress updates, new solution offerings that might be relevant, industry knowledge and expertise, etc., in their efforts to be viewed as a strategic thought leader and trusted advisor.

In addition, these concepts also benefit those responsible for *finding new business*, in more of a true prospecting or *hunter* type mode, within targeted prospect or client opportunities that have been identified as potentially lucrative.

Finally, this material applies to those who find themselves in the ever so fortunate position of responding to an RFP (request for proposal) or RFI (request for information). Better yet, these principles can help craft a value proposition that may in fact head off—or eliminate altogether—the need on the client's part for an RFP. And *that* ought to make you smile.

INTRODUCTION

Welcome—and thank you for picking up this book. It's been a long time coming—20 years of experience as an entrepreneur, before offering something that could be referenced for years to come.

I have attempted to share some ideas and concepts I hope you will find beneficial in your business life—perhaps even in your personal life. These concepts have paid significant dividends for our clients, and my sincere hope is that they will provide similar benefits for you and your organization.

All of us have purchased things that—from time-to-time, didn't measure up to what we were hoping. I'd like this book to be the opposite of that experience, by having you put these concepts to use, finding true value as a result. That—is my goal.

With this in mind, I'd like to share the core principles upon which these concepts are based, and the vision for what we hope this book will bring to you and your organization, and to those with whom you interact.

These principles are simple, unsophisticated, genuine and timeless. However, I sense a genuine need on all of our parts to heed them more than perhaps we do.

Respectfulness—honesty—fairness—stewardship—simple courteousness—directness—becoming more worthy—and excellent ethics.

—Being more respectful of the other, more courteous, and worthy of their time. Being a better steward, by educating yourself about their business, their industry, and their own internal "goings-on", before ever attempting to engage them. And being more honoring, by learning about their current challenges, goals and objectives;

then looking *inward* at the products, services, and solutions your organization brings to bear, doing your best to help them understand what real value you could bring—*if* they were to engage with you and your organization.

These are the principles upon which the methodologies are based. They are grounded and centered with these core values in mind. So if they resonate with you, you will find this material of value for your enterprise.

Here's how we look at this topic. All of us *sell*. We are all, from time-to-time, trying to sell or influence other people—trying to get our children, a brother or sister, or our friends to do something. Or we're trying to sell an idea, a desire, feeling, or cause we believe in. And let's not forget those of us who *sell* for a living—like the millions of people who provide for themselves and their families by selling a product, service, or some type of solution.

In my opinion, most of us don't do a very good job of communicating to those we are trying to influence, the answers to two simple questions:

1. *Why are we worthy of their time and attention?*
2. *What is the real value that we, or our "stuff",*
   really provide to them?

And because most of us are not very good at doing this, it actually makes it a difficult and *undesirable hassle* for those we are trying so hard to influence. In fact, we—by our lack of clarity, actually add to their *irritation factor*. And in one sense—this can be viewed as being disrespectful of those you wish to influence. It's hard to be a respectful, good steward of other people's time, when you make them *"work-like-a-dog"* to figure out why they *should* pay attention, why they need you, and how you can truly help them.

So if you agree, then improving your ability to *crystallize, condense* and *articulate* the real value that your capabilities, products, services, and solutions bring to another organization—the more respectful, courteous, and helpful you become. And isn't *that* what it's all about?

One of the goals of this material is to foster a renewed commitment and focus toward these principles by following the concepts in the coming chapters.

This book has been designed for senior executives—CEOs and Presidents, EVP, SVP, and VPs of Business Divisions such as Sales and Business Development, Strategic Growth, Marketing, Customer Service, and Training and Organizational Development for organizations of all sizes, public and private. Managers, Supervisors, and of course the sales organization, will also benefit from this material.

Finally, it is for owners and entrepreneurs who perhaps *do* have a great product, service, or solution that might truly be outstanding. But the fact is, nobody cares! Why? —*Because their value proposition has no TEETH.*

Either there is no value proposition to start with—they don't know how to put one together, or the one they have simply says nothing—really. *It has no TEETH. It is mush.* In fact, in years of helping companies shape, condense or recalibrate their value propositions, it has been our experience that initially, most companies think their message is pretty good—until they invest the time to really address what they are saying to their target audiences, and discover that it's not that *tight, clear, or compelling.*

If this is the case for your enterprise, then *your message commands no attention*—and *pulls no one toward you.* It also creates *no sense of urgency* with those prospects or existing clients whom you'd love to spend more time with. Instead they appear *totally uninterested* in you—your message—and your offerings. When this happens, most of us get nervous—not to mention that sales cycles stretch, cost of sales goes up, and margins get hammered because you get *shopped*.

Whether you're a multi-national corporation, a mid-sized or smaller business, this book can provide significant take-home value if you apply the core principles to your business.

Thank you and enjoy the book.

Michael A. Boylan

CHAPTER ONE
Let's Define it, Shall We—Your Value Proposition

What is One?

I could attempt to impress you with some complex, scholarly sounding textbook definition, dazzling you with my intellectual grasp of this subject matter—but I don't have one really. My definition instead, is based on 20 plus years of "on the street" and "in the field—doing it" street smarts in what has worked, and what will not work going forward.

A value proposition is a well packaged—condensed—ultra-clear statement to your target audience, that communicates the answers to: If "they" do business with you or your organization, you will help them to do—or they will receive:

- This:_____
  _____

- This, and _____
  _____

- This:_____
  _____

You're the one who needs to fill in the blanks. What do I mean?

Many organizations, (even some top producers), are too darn fuzzy, garbled, and unclear about *why* another organization should do business with them. Meaning, they can't explain quickly or concisely, the answers to; *"If we engage in a relationship with your company—what can we expect to get or experience—exactly—or within a general range?"*

A value proposition is not your organization's sales pitch or "shtick". It is the climax or culmination of the pitch—the *net-net*—the *big bat* that you lead with, that can effectively hit the prospect or client with a clear, compelling, and on-point statement—calibrated to a specific targeted company, audience, or vertical—that communicates very concisely, *"If you do business with us, we can, through our product, service, or solution offerings, help your organization to:*

1. _____
   _____
   _____

2. _____
   _____
   _____

3. _____
   _____
   _____

Yes this is hard. We know that. But your ability to condense your message into a tightly packaged, "beautifully wrapped" statement, (or two or three)—that defines the core essence of what the prospect or client can expect to receive—is critical to your continued success going forward.

This allows your target audience to pull softly at the golden bow that's so concisely *wrapped* around your value proposition—so that it unfolds into their hearts and minds in a concise message that they don't have to *work* to understand or figure out.

It's very clear as to what they'll get if they engage or do business with your organization. The clearer you are, the better your opportunities for credible access to the levels of executives you desire more face time with, so you can close more business at a faster pace. That's what a good value proposition is, and what it can do for your organization.

Why Do I Need One?

Well perhaps you don't. It really depends on the levels of access you're wanting to attain. In the U.S. for example, director, manager, and lower levels of management typically aren't bothered if you don't hit them between the eyes with a tightly condensed value proposition. Why? Because many don't think that way. Some, unfortunately, don't even care. They would rather focus on the *minutia* of your offerings. This is gradually changing however, because they have more choices available to them.

In the near future, these individuals will begin to force you into a tighter space, a tighter message—a value proposition, as demands on their time grow; the number of vendor choices continues to expand—and there is less and less *real* product, service, or solution differentiation among the choices presented to them.

Now if your desired target audience within a given organization— be it a new prospect or existing client, is *up-radar* within that firm—perhaps a National Director, Vice President or Division President, Senior or Executive Vice President, Chief Operating Officer, Chief Technology Officer, or President/CEO—then a tightly calibrated and condensed value proposition is *mandatory*. It is a flat-out *must* if you expect to get their attention, and gain access to them, so you can present your message and solution offerings to an audience who can actually make a decision without an "Act of Congress."

Many clients we have worked with over the years express that decisions—sometimes even basic decisions—are coming slower, while committees, task forces, and the number of outside consultants involved in *the process* are getting larger by the day. We whole-heartedly agree. What this points to, is the heightened necessity for a crisp, clear, well-articulated and well-understood value proposition if you expect to reduce your closing cycles and maintain or improve your margins. It is very important for all of us.

Why Else Do I Need One?

Here are a few more reasons why:

—You'll gain access faster and earlier on in your selling cycle, to those people you *want* access to.

—Prospects and customers are in a state of *information overload* all of the time. And don't kid yourself. *All* vendor options look "vanilla" to them. They also *believe* that you're offerings are not *that* much *different*, or *better* than any of their other options.

—Nowadays, prospects and clients truly *feel* and *believe* that most people are unclear, imprecise, take too long to get to the point, and often can't even articulate *their key points of difference*. This creates a downward spiral where they feel that whoever is coming at them asking for access, is not really worthy of their time yet, or perhaps ever. They also believe that *they* can "cut the wheat from the chaff" much faster than any salesperson or business developer can. And on goes the downward spiral.

—Nowadays, prospects and clients have several *legitimate* options, vendors, solutions, choices—call it whatever you'd like. The power pendulum has totally swung around. ***They are in control! They are driving the bus—not you!*** Therefore, senior executives, sales and business developers, entrepreneurs and organizations that are crystal clear at explaining *visually*, in layman's terms, *earlier on in their approach*—what their value propositions are, will have a greater probability of gaining access to the correct audiences at a more rapid pace. Hence, the more they increase their chances of closing opportunities.

—There has been a massive *increase in fear, uncertainty*, and a dramatic *reduction of trust and loyalties* among those whom you'd like access to, between senior management and mid-management, and mid-management and the line workforce. Most of these individuals are also skeptical of anyone attempting to gain access to them, meaning you and your producers.

There are several more points I could offer, but you get the point. *Get real clear on helping your people answer these questions:*

"Why in the heck does our organization need you and your stuff? Why should we care—really? What's the net-net?"

Start focusing all of what you bring to the table—all of your products, services and solutions—and start driving toward the answers to:

"That's nice—so what. Why should we care about that?"

Can I Get Along Without One?

The short answer is, *"How long would you like to have success in business?"* No, you can't get along without one! People in general, naturally gravitate towards others who are clear, "plain-languaged", crisp and condensed communicators; people they can understand. Why would you want to put forth a *mushy* value proposition that a prospect or client could blow holes in, until you drop out of the sky—arrive dead on arrival, and were never *heard*—all because your messages were so darn confusing?

So now *you* answer the question. Can you and your enterprise get along without a clear, condensed, and tightly calibrated value proposition, and expect to grow your business profitably?

In the last few years, there has been a significant paradigm shift in *when* and *how* business professionals want to hear your condensed messages and value propositions.

For years, the common thinking has been "just get in" at *whatever* level—just take the meeting—start learning—ask the right questions—gain an understanding of their needs and goals, listen and clarify; build that all important *rapport*—ask more brilliant questions such as, "*So what keeps you up at night?*" — take intensive notes like you're working your tail off, etc., etc.

Well nowadays—the *vibe* and *push-back* coming from the prospect is, "*You know what—I'm not interested in educating you as to what we're trying to do around here, until you can tell me first—quickly and concisely, in a fashion that I can understand, 'if I do business with you and your organization—what do we get, or exactly how is that going to help us?' Answer that—and maybe I'll let you in, to share the business problems we'd like help solving.*"

In summary, can *you and your producers* get along without one? There is only one answer, and the answer is no.

Mine's Been Just Fine For Years

Translation? *"Our message and story are just fine. They seemed to have worked for us over the years, so we don't need to tweak them. They're very clear. Plus, our sales people know how to articulate them once they're in."*

If this describes your thinking, you may be playing *"access roulette"*. And we wish you luck in getting access to those executives your producers desire an audience with, because it will rarely happen as quickly as you would like.

Perhaps this is dim thinking. If your sales cycles are stretching, your cost of sales is on the rise, your margins are shrinking in certain areas of your business, and if there is an angst or general frustration among your producers, where their attitude toward prospects and clients is, "they just don't get it—they're totally missing the point of how we can help them," then may we suggest ever so politely that perhaps *you and your sales people are the ones missing the point*. It is our hope that your senior leadership and sales/business development organization will be open to shaping tighter, more focused messages and value propositions.

Allow me to state it another way. One of the key goals of a sales professional, or anyone in business for that matter, has always been to just "get in the door". Start learning and listening, clarifying, qualifying, and *earning* credibility and rapport, as you go through the process of learning what the prospect or client really wants, needs, and can afford. Then you can shape the best solution offerings to address those objectives.

Nowadays, what has become all too real is that most prospects, *even existing clients, are much less interested in giving you the time or the luxury to learn about their needs, goals and objectives.*

Instead—*before they determine whether they will meet with you* or your producers, they first want the answers to the following questions spelled out concisely:

1. A condensed and compelling, well-articulated value proposition(s) stating exactly how your offerings could help them—which needs to include the answers to, *"For how much—how fast—by when—what's the probability or ratio that you can actually deliver—and who have you done this for?"*

2. Why you are worthy of an audience, and why *should* you be let in?

3. If we let you in, how will you use your time, what's your agenda, and what are you going to cover?

4. If we're happy with meeting number one, then what? What's the next step? Where are you driving me? What's "the process"? What am I signing up for?

Now can you and your business developers answer all of these questions? Or better yet, are they answering them now? Our guess is, maybe not, even though the answers to these questions are paramount.

In summary, let's assume that your value propositions are not *just fine* for the time being. Instead let's assume—at least while we go through this book—that they could be improved to provide better results for your enterprise.

CHAPTER TWO

The Trends—and Why You Should Take a Hard Look at Your Value Propositions

Your Value Proposition—Consider a Re-Torque

If you're a President, CEO, business owner, executive, senior or vice president of sales, business development, or any other business unit—consider filling in your answers in the grid on the next page. It will help you assess how your current process really works.

We challenge you to *block and tackle out your current sales process* specifically, from start to finish.

We recommend you answer this matrix, not with how things *should work*—but how they *actually do work inside your organization*. (A hint: you may want your sales director's, manager's, area or regional vice president's help completing this matrix. And don't be surprised if your team doesn't know, or can't agree on some of the answers.)

Block and Tackle Out Your Current Sales Process

(Note: Fill one out for prospect opportunities—another for current clients. See if there are any differences between them).

In conference call, in-person, or meeting #	*How many people are typically in attendance?*	*What are the titles of those in the room, or involved?*	*What's the message communicated? What is actually taking place?*	*What's the typical result of the meeting or interaction?*
1				
2				
3				
4				
5				
6				
7				
8				
9				
10				
11				
12				

After you have completed the matrix, think about and answer these three questions:

1. **At whom are your current messages and value propositions aimed?**

2. **Is that the same audience you and your sales professionals are typically successful in gaining access to? And if so...**

3. **What percentage of the time?**

Based on experience with clients, *there is usually some slippage in this area of an organization's sales and business development process.*

If this is the case in your enterprise, we hope you'll be open to a re-torque, meaning a **condensing**—a **reshaping**—and a **recalibration** of your value proposition(s), to be more aligned to the levels of access you and your producers want more exposure to. More on how to do this in the chapters to come.

Ultra Hyper Combative Competition

Many of us compete and do business in a pretty intense, sometimes combative landscape. Hence, a well-shaped, properly wordsmithed value proposition has actually helped our clients close larger deals, earlier on in their selling process. Why? Because it has allowed them to be *heard* at more senior executive levels within the client or prospect organization, sometimes faster than their competitors. This provides for the beginnings of discussions and relationships at levels where people have more power and authority to make decisions faster. And often, the competition isn't there.

Senior executives, as you know, can pull monies from other *buckets*, perhaps even shut down the *need* to do an exhaustive request for proposal (RFP) or request for information (RFI)—which usually leads to the creation of a committee or task force. And if you're really fortunate, the *outside consulting firm* will shepherd along the whole *creation of the requirements*. This usually leads to a matrix, used to *grade* vendor responses and site demos, which can add months, sometimes years to your selling cycle, all before you even get an answer. This increases your selling costs... not to mention that lucky-strike extra—*your margins get hammered in the process*. You get the point.

"You're a Commodity Too—Basically—Aren't You?"

Here is yet another major reason in support of tightening down your message and value proposition(s).

Prospects, and for that matter, many of your clients *truly believe* there is so little *real difference* between your suite of offerings and the three or four other pretty good choices they have, that they're beginning to view your offerings, along with your direct competitors' as, *"Well—they're all about the same. They're all pretty good, experience wise, feature-benefit wise, cost wise, ROI wise, and service and support wise. In many respects, each solution could probably serve our needs."*

In fact, as you're about to set up a meeting, you may hear them say something like this, *"Do you have a brochure or some information you could forward to us? You see, we're very interested, but before we take a meeting with you, our people, in fact, my people—need to sort through this stuff, so we can make some initial judgment calls on who we should meet with. So just hang in there; send us your stuff, and we'll be in touch."* These statements prove the point.

And it's statements like these that drive most of us crazy. Personally, these are early signals that you may already be *toast*, or that you have a *very long selling process* ahead.

The more your targeted prospects and clients view your offerings as a *commodity play*, the tougher it can be for your business, and the easier it is for them to push you and your business developers into the *basement* of their organization. Why? Because they believe there's no *need* to be involved in the initial "courting" process—at least at their level.

Instead, lucky you. The committee or task force will sort it all out over the next 6-18 months. In this case, I hope you have deep pockets and tons of patience because it will take a while. And it's pretty hard to speed *the process* along, once the task force gets assembled. Instead, it's like stepping into quicksand. If you've got ten people on the task force—that's usually ten sets of opinions to deal with right?

The solution to this *commodity* type attitude and perception is to "get in" at higher levels, where they don't care as much about the *minutia* of the offerings. Instead, they care much more about *the big picture stuff*.

The End of — "We're a Significant Player in Our Space" —So Dig Us Man

I know the old, *"No One Ever Got Fired For Buying IBM"*, has played really well. But today and tomorrow that thinking holds much less promise in an ultra competitive global economy.

Of course market dominance is powerful, attractive, and often an easy way out of a complex decision process, but for what levels of decision makers? The answer is usually for mid to lower levels of people within an organization.

However, what if a *renegade cowboy* or *cowgirl*—a vice president, senior vice president, executive vice president, chief financial officer, chief information officer or chief executive—is involved in the decision process? My opinion—be a little more cautious.

In this scenario, don't be so quick to puff out your chest with the, *"We're the number 1, 2, or 3 player in our space"* pitch. Why? Because the trends more and more are suggesting that, to some of these self-proclaimed *hot-shot* senior executives, that doesn't mean as much anymore. Why? Because they'd have *less control over you and your organization* (if you represent a large player) and that's actually *bad* in their opinion. Do you see where we're headed?

These top guns often want maximum control and leverage over you, the vendor. Often, we coach our clients to disregard their comments such as, *"We're looking for true partnerships with our vendors and suppliers."* That, in many instances is *fluff*. They instead want to play you off against the other vendors, and that's a bit harder to do when you're one of the top three or four providers.

So if this is the case for you and your company, being a major player could end up biting you in the back side, depending on the levels at which you are engaged. Therefore, watch your level of confidence, even if you do have major market dominance in your space. Remember what Andy Grove, CEO of Intel has said, *"Only the paranoid survive."*

Everyone say "Vanilla"—Then Get Upset When You Lose

Have you bought a VCR, DVD, or some kind of electronic toy in the last 12 months from one of those giant superstores? If so, can you picture yourself standing there, arms folded, glazing at the little orange or yellow plastic feature and benefit marquees along side about 15-20 different brands, as you slowly begin to say to yourself, "O.K., for VCRs there's:

—JVC...3 heads, 90 day warranty, $299.95, etc., etc.
—Pioneer...3 heads, 90 day warranty, $339.95, etc., etc.
—Sony...4 heads, 120 day warranty, $379.95, etc., etc.
—Mitsubishi...2 heads, 30 days service, $295.00, etc., etc.
—Toshiba... 4 heads, 12 month warranty, $589.95, etc., etc.

As you stand there and compare, don't you quickly say to yourself, *"You know, they're all about the same?"* Even if you had each company's representative standing next to their product, pitching you until they're blue in the face, that their product is by far and away totally superior. The *truth* is—in your mind—your perception is, *"They're all pretty close—they're all pretty good—they'd all do the job—and they're all about the same."*

Therefore, perception becomes reality, and any *minor* key points of difference that your offerings may very well have over your competition, gets drowned out with white noise. *Remember—the perception always wins. It's really "vanilla!"*

Welcome to how your prospects—perhaps even some of your existing customers, may view your organization, and your product, service and solution offerings!

All the more reason to put some serious time, energy, and focused attention toward creating some *ultra-clear* value propositions that rock, and allow your producers access at *50,000 feet.*

CHAPTER THREE
Why Do So Many Say Nothing? Can You Say "Mush"?

There are many reasons why so many value propositions are *mush*. Typically, most sales producers and persuaders in general, have their heads down, focused on the wonderful whistles and bells, features, and maybe a few benefits of their offerings, versus concentrating on what all of these things *combined*, deliver to the prospect or customer, in regards to true value.

The majority of sales and business development professionals, *even many senior executives*, often have a hard time explaining clearly, in a condensed fashion, the true value that their *stuff* really winds up delivering to the prospect or client.

To take it one step further, most producers rarely wind up in the senior executive suite, early in their sales process (if ever), so they're not used to being forced or crunched into communicating what their value propositions are by a senior executive. Therefore, most producers don't even *think* this way. Instead, they're used to *the chat*. They're used to asking fabulously brilliant and insightful questions such as, *"So now—what do you guys do then here anyway, huh? Can you tell me a little bit about your business so that I can learn how we might be able to help you?"*

This question usually irritates senior executives, sending them into orbit. They are hardly interested in *the chat*. They instead want to be hit over the head with a compelling, condensed, *machine-gun blast* with the answers to: *"How exactly can you help us, and why should I care?"* Unfortunately, most professionals don't know how to do this. What's even more dangerous is, many are not even sure why it's so important.

Because so many business professionals are not *practiced* at delivering their messages to senior executives or owners, they naturally don't *think* like senior officers or owners. And they aren't practiced, because they don't get much training in how to take all of the things that they market, sell, or promote, and condense them into a few bullet points that articulate the true value that all of their *stuff* really delivers for a client organization. Therefore, if you're on the receiving end of one of their presentations, it does sound like *"mush."* And in some cases, *"mega-mush."*

To be fair though, let's also turn our attention to senior executives for a moment. We have come across a few who have been arrogant, lazy, and out of touch with how difficult it has become to get in the door at senior executive levels. In fact, some frankly don't understand what you're talking about when you ask them what their value propositions are. Or worse yet, why a good one is so necessary nowadays.

Therefore, it's really not that surprising that so many say nothing. It's uncharted water for many senior executives and their sales and marketing organizations.

No One's In a Hurry But You and Your Organization

Most of us represent pretty good stuff—pretty good ideas, products, services, and solution offerings. The problem is—*so does everybody else.*

You can fixate all day long on how great your offerings are, in terms of how they can benefit prospects and clients. However, in most industries and businesses, prospects and clients more than likely have at least 3-5 *other* pretty good options, in addition to yours. Therefore, they are *rarely* in a hurry to get with you and your people anymore— even though you're *usually* in a hurry to meet with them.

Need some proof? When was the last time you connected with someone over the phone, and heard them say, *"Where have you been? Why haven't you called me? Get in here! We need to meet!"*

Unless you've invented some new *thing* and the market is coming after you (usually a short-lived reality anyway), it is not normal to have prospects or customers lined up at our door in desperate need to talk with us. So if that's the way it is for you and your producers, this value proposition stuff is critical to your organization's success going forward.

Did You Expect "Your People" to Figure it Out?

I'm addressing owners, entrepreneurs and senior level executives for a moment—but everyone else—please dial in.

In our strategic consulting work, we find the *norm* to be that many of these individuals usually think their message(s) and value propositions are pretty clear—*"crystal clear"*, to quote Jack Nicholson's character in the movie *A Few Good Men*.

However, more often than not, they haven't communicated *what* the value propositions are, to the real message carriers, meaning the sales and business development organization. And even when they have taken the time to do so, what is common is, the producers don't *understand* or *believe* them—or worse yet, think they are total *fluff*. Unfortunately, we see this a good bit.

And because many entrepreneurs and senior executives feel their message and value propositions are clear, correct, well-defined and well-stated, they usually believe it's the sales producers who don't "get it", or are simply not too sharp.

We get nervous when we find owners and senior executives who *allow* their sales people to "figure out" what the messages and value propositions *should be*, on their own—without much direction, input or advice from the top. When this happens, it is a sure-fire recipe for even more *mush*.

It is interesting when we hear senior executives say, ***"You know, I really don't know exactly what the messages and value propositions are that the sales people are carrying forward, but as long as they continue to make their numbers, I really don't care. It's whatever works!"***

If this describes your organization, even if it's difficult to admit, we urge you to improve in this area of business by taking this topic seriously. Help yourself, your business developers and your company, by drilling down to the key financial net benefits and key points of difference that your organization, *and* your suite of offerings bring to the table. They need to be measurable, quantifiable, and honest. In fact, a framework will be provided in Chapter Seven, to help you begin doing this.

In summary, *your people* can't and shouldn't be left to figure this stuff out on their own. It can be complex, therefore, it takes a concerted effort from the top to the bottom of the organization. Hence, we recommend rolling up your sleeves and getting busy—as a team.

Zero Harmony—Lot's of Plaque

Even if you believe how important this skill set really is, and even if you're "gung-ho" on wanting to improve your own, most people want and need *hard-core reasons* for *why they should* do this or that. And since change can be hard—and because we're all busy— most people *really don't move on anything* until there is some sort of *consequence* presented, be it real or perceived.

That being said, here are some questions that may spur you to think about what it's like inside your own organization. Assume for a moment that your company's message and value propositions are clear, articulate, and easily understood by prospects and clients— they are clear as a bell.

With that as a given, would you agree that everyone inside your organization should be able to communicate your company's value propositions in the same way, or would that not apply to you?

And—if you did have one unified message that truly articulated what all of your products, services and solutions delivered to the customer, do you believe that everyone inside your organization *would*, *could* or *should* communicate this unified message in the same cohesive manner? Or would the *norm* inside your company be—the senior executives have their *own* way of explaining the business you're in, and the value you bring to the customer? The marketing department has *their* own unique *spin* on how they like to communicate "the message." And the directors and managers? Well sometimes unfortunately, they weren't even a part of the discussion in creating the message, so they're a little offended and upset. Therefore, they may not even buy into this sharp new value proposition. Instead, *they create their own*—on the fly, that *they* believe best suits their own needs much better—bruised ego and all.

Throw in the sales professionals—often some of the best *hip shooters* on the face of the planet—who choose not to be *pinned down* on how they explain or articulate the value proposition—since they usually prefer to craft something on the spur of the moment, when backed into a corner by a prospect or customer.

As these scenarios are presented, which one is closer to your situation? Is it standard operating procedure that everyone from the top to the bottom of your organization is in harmony—singing the same song, on the same key, at the same time, with the same pronunciation and diction? Or is it more like there is no harmony inside your company when it comes to communicating your value propositions?

If you choose to invest the financial resources, time, effort and mental bandwidth to attempt to craft a condensed and meaningfully articulate set of value proposition(s) that the whole organization can be proud of, and communicate concisely, then be aware that it will take a concerted effort to *get* and *keep* everyone singing in six part harmony.

As you may agree, many companies do not control or manage very well, many of their most important *touch points* with current clients, prospects, or key vertical industry sectors in which they do business. This includes everything from basic conversations with prospects and clients, to local or national media or public relations announcements, basic emails, direct mail, brochures, websites, and product, service or solution literature. It also includes more spendy avenues such as print, radio and television advertising, and elaborate corporate events.

The *norm* seems to have become—each event—or each product or service—has a different message, and a different brochure or direct mail piece, with little *cohesion* around the central value proposition. Rarely, do product/service brochures or website descriptions tie together the company's central value proposition in a common and consistent manner.

Therefore, it's pretty easy to understand the recipient of the messages' frustration and confusion. Not only is your prospect or client a roving target, but *you*—the one who is trying to sell something— are also a roving target, sharing nothing but mush and confusion. This is the case when you don't offer your audience a *unified, buttoned-down, cohesive,* and *consistent message* in all of your various touch points, mediums and channels of communication. It just becomes one huge barrier to good business health, which we call ***plaque***.

Gum Disease is Always a Possibility

Getting your *teeth* cleaned every six months is a good start toward maintaining healthy *teeth* and gums. So in one sense, you could compare it to working on your value propositions and arriving at something you, your colleagues and employees all seem to like. But the work starts now. If you don't brush regularly, floss, and keep up the general health of communicating your new value propositions in a consistent manner—what good have you done yourself? And if you let things slide, *gum disease* inside your organization, especially within the sales and business development organization, is always a possibility at any time.

Based on what we see, the norm is that several in management rarely have a consistent or cohesive value proposition to share, let alone train their people on how to deliver it. So plaque begins to form between you, your company and the prospect or client. And it continues to get *thicker* until you blast it away with a value proposition that has *TEETH.*

If you are going to lay blame anywhere in this scenario, place it at the top of the organization. These are the individuals who are supposed to be "showing the troops the way", partly through a cohesive value proposition.

Therefore, getting key players in your organization from senior management, to the sales and business development organization, marketing, customer service, and other touch points, singing in harmony—is necessary if you wish to grow, maintain, or not slide backwards. Remember, *anyone is a candidate for gum disease at any time, regardless of the size of your organization.*

We will share more about how and why you might want to cascade your value propositions across all touch points in Chapter Nine.

CHAPTER FOUR
Senior Management Buffaloes Themselves

The Arrogance Drag on Your Selling Cycle

In this complex and sometimes goofy business world, it's become easier for a senior executive inside a large or mid-sized company to hide, avoid responsibility, and not get too worried about whether it's a worthwhile exercise to invest the time, money and effort to make sure the sales and business development organization is carrying forward and communicating the right messages and value propositions to prospects and existing clients.

However—rest assured they get more serious about this topic when their stock takes a nose dive, stays flat for a number of quarters, or gets downgraded by an institution or analyst. And you *know* they're more attentive when they miss their revenue targets for the quarter, or for the year.

This is what we call *buffaloing yourself*—having the opinion that things are fine until a financial hiccup occurs. Remember, we're all busy, and many people are reactive. Unfortunately, a consequence usually has to occur before people pay attention and take things more seriously.

But one doesn't have to fall into this category. If you think about it, what is more important to your organization's success than being able to articulate the right messages and value propositions to the correct audiences to whom you desire more access or exposure? Our answer. Nothing.

"When I Sold, You Just Called the Guy Up and..."

If you are an owner, entrepreneur, or senior level executive and have found yourself saying, (either to your sales producers or sales managers), *"Well back when I sold, you just called the guy up and talked to him. It's as simple as that."* If you have said something like this, we suggest you do the following:

Pick up the phone and dial the number of a senior executive that one of your sales producers would like to talk with, or get in to see. Then try to get that individual on the phone so you can *just talk to him/her.* And if you succeed, see how long you can keep that person on the phone. Repeat this exercise five more times, and you will begin to see that times have changed. It's not as easy anymore to just "reach out and touch someone".

Reality Blast—Back to the Street Please

It is inevitable that as we get older, we sometimes lose some of our quickness, spark, maybe even our edge. As we make more money, it can become easier to let some of the skills that helped us become successful, slip a bit.

Even though you may have been able to throw a touchdown pass, or serve up *aces* in business in prior years, doesn't mean you'll continue on with the same levels of accuracy and success for as long as you're on the field or court.

Because the playing field of executive level access, and of calibrating the right message and value propositions to the right audience(s) has changed so much, we suggest you jump in with both feet and hit the street. Get your senior sales management and producers together and talk with them. Ask them what's *blocking* them, slowing them down, causing deals to *stall* or go *sideways*, or preventing them from gaining access to the audiences they desire.

If you listen attentively and try to understand their responses, you may be surprised with what they have to say. Then as you begin to understand where your own organization's gaps may be, begin "chunking-out" the core aspects of your message that you feel must be heard by those whom you desire more access and exposure to.

CHAPTER FIVE
What Does Your Value Proposition Say? Does It Pull? From Whom?

To Whom Are You Trying to Appeal and Get In Front of?

A good way to begin this empowering and high-dollar-return process is to look at your current messages or value propositions as they are now. Then answer these questions:

Question 1: What does your existing product, service, solution, corporate message or value proposition really say? Is it honest and measurable, or does it cause you to say, *"So what?"* Be honest.

_____

_____

_____

Question 2: Is it compelling, and does it cut through the fluff? This should be a fast answer.

_____

_____

_____

Question 3: What *types* of people are your message(s) pulling toward you and your company? What levels of executives does it attract, and from what types of companies?

_____

_____

_____

Question 4: Are these the levels of executives, and types of companies to whom you desire access? If not, to whom *exactly* do you need to appeal? What levels of executives, and what companies do you want to talk with more frequently?

Question 5: If *you* were one of the target executives you were trying to attract, what would your message or value proposition need to communicate, in order to cause *you* to pay attention and grant somebody access to you? Think about this for a minute before you answer.

If you are at all concerned as you attempted to answer these questions, don't be. Know that this is complex and sometimes just plain hard. Why? Because the business world is more complex, and because prospects and clients have many more excellent choices. And the *noise* and confusion factor are at all time highs. But not to worry—the *noise* will get even louder in the years ahead. All the more reason to get real clear—real fast.

Define What Levels it Should Speak to—by Titles Please

Continuing on—you, your producers, and senior leaders must decide exactly who you want to talk with. *Don't leave it up to your prospect or client to decide.* Meaning, what titles inside your target organizations, what levels of individuals do you want in front of your producers? For that matter, what titles do you want to avoid so that your sales cycles don't drag on forever?

It will help if you think through, then complete the following questions:

Question A: What are the titles of the individuals you desire in meeting number one? Define why.

_____

_____

_____

Question B: What are the titles of the individuals you do not want in meeting number one? Define why.

_____

_____

_____

Question C: Define by title, the levels of executives your message and value propositions are *supposed* to speak to? Then do your own self-assessment. Do they—or do they not?

_____

_____

_____

In summary—select your target audience(s) by the titles/levels of executives you want to appeal and attract toward you first, as you begin to shape, re-torque, and recalibrate your messages and value propositions.

CHAPTER SIX
What's a Good Value Proposition Supposed to Do?

The Elements of a Great One

A great value proposition gives you the access and exposure you desire—be it a face-to-face, conference call, video conference or email access, to the levels of executives you desire, at the time in which you need or want the access, *so that you can present your message/value propositions in the exact manner in which you wish to present them*. That's it—plain and simple. That's what a good one should do.

This means that it must communicate what we like to call the *"net-net"* of what all of your *offerings* can bring to bear on the prospect or existing client's behalf.

It must *summarize the core results* of what all of your products, services, solution offerings, credentials, skill sets and experience can deliver for the client. All of these elements should be rolled up into a few snappy, bullet-point statements that speak to the levels of executives you're after. It must draw them to you. This is what a good one can and will do.

If you're going to ask, *"Good. Are you going to tell me exactly how to build mine, and exactly what it should say?"* The answer is, it's not possible at this point. We would need specific background knowledge on your business, your offerings, how they benefit clients, and by how much, whom you want access to, and why they should pay attention? However, the core advice and guidelines we are providing can provide excellent payoff, if you and your producers use them. In fact, you may decide as you attempt these exercises, to request some assistance.

We have built a track record of doing precisely this for Fortune 1000 and mid-sized organizations. It's challenging, mind-bending, strategic, and mentally like a chess-game—creating a road-map—a front-end process for:

A.   Attracting the correct levels of executives earlier on in the selling process, so clients can better *control* the environment in which they present their value propositions.

B.   Helping determine what they should *lead* with, to gain the access and exposure desired.

C.   Helping determine *exactly* what they want the next step to be, if meeting number one goes well.

Some clients believe this work belongs at the *front end* of their existing sales process, and we agree.

Our questions to you are: *"Where are you driving your prospect or client? What exactly do you want them to do next, if your first meeting is successful?"* We call this thought process, *Driving The Bus*™.

If you think about your existing selling process, I would wager a guess that *your prospects **and** your clients are driving your bus!*

This thought process, if taken seriously, can help you drive your own bus—so that *you and your producers* control the *speed, direction*, and *ultimate destination* of each prospect and client encounter. This is very important if you wish to *collapse* your organization's selling and closing cycles.

The work we have done for clients in this arena has helped drive significant additional top-line revenues, reduced their cost of sales by collapsing their selling cycles—improving the margin on deals closed. These financial benefits are very exciting for companies.

The Chameleon Always Wins—Always the Tweak

We categorize value propositions in two camps:

1. **The Generic Capabilities Value Proposition**—that you can use on most prospects and existing clients, and

2. **The Custom Shaped Value Proposition**—which addresses more specifically how your value proposition(s) can impact the prospect or client's self-stated needs, goals, and objectives as stated in their annual report, 10K, 10Q, or the research you've sourced.

What is the ideal? It is to have your value proposition(s) address *both* camps, so that the individuals you're attempting access to know you've done your homework on their organization, and their goals and objectives.

This creates the *feeling* in those whom you're attempting to engage, that perhaps you are more *worthy*, because you are attempting to be a *respectful steward* of their time, by sourcing the research, learning *"who the players are"* inside their organization, what they are trying to accomplish and by when, etc. Then communicating exactly how you could help them and their business.

For those who prefer definitions, they are as follows:

1. **The Generic Capabilities Value Proposition**
   A broad-sweeping and generic, yet concise statement, (or two or three) as to how your organization's offerings could benefit the prospect or client. Hopefully these statements have *TEETH*, meaning financial metrics, which we'll discuss shortly.

2. The Custom-Shaped Value Proposition

These are specific value propositions calibrated to explain how your organization or suite of offerings can help solve the prospect's or client's self-stated goals, objectives, and challenges. These statements should be customized for each organization you target. In our experience, the tighter these messages are calibrated, the better your opportunity for senior executive level access and *real* rapport.

Our coaching is this: In order to become more worthy of access, and to be a respectful steward of their time, become a better *"tweaker"* of your value propositions.

Does it Have TEETH—or is it a Gumby?

The elements of a cohesive, concise, and articulate value proposition circle around one big topic which is—**the financial metrics—the TEETH**.

Simply speaking, in financial layman's terms; *"Just exactly what does your suite of offerings —rolled-up—really deliver, bottom-line? And how will it impact and affect my organization?"* You would be surprised to learn the names of some of the corporations that cannot articulate how their offerings financially benefit their own clients', bottom-line. However, in all honesty, *most organizations wrestle with this challenge.*

Either their products, services, and solutions have been relatively *easy* to sell, or competition hasn't been a factor, that they've been able to get along without having to come up with their own financial benefit metrics. What's even more common among companies is, *many don't know how much their offerings have impacted the client organization, because most often, no one has ever taken the time to measure, quantify, or track the financial impact—they'll say they can't—or that their clients won't share the data.*

Therefore, when senior executives "pound their fists" asking for some statement or benchmark telling them *just how much* your offerings could impact their business, many companies throw up their hands and guesstimate! Nothing wrong with that. However, we are living in an ultra-competitive, sometimes combative business world. Since most prospects and clients have at least three other *pretty good choices* for almost every product, service or solution on the planet, our thinking is:

Those organizations who can measure, quantify, prove, or explain precisely, or within a general range how much their product, service, or solutions can, or have financially benefited their clients—they will have the keys to controlling their organization's financial destiny.

For those who cannot get their arms around how much their offerings can financially impact a client, don't worry. You can still develop a good value proposition that will benefit you. We just thought it would help you to see the view from the *50,000 foot level*—meaning how a CEO, CFO, CIO, COO or other senior level executives may view you and your value propositions—if you cannot articulate *one of the most important core elements of a good value proposition*—in their eyes. And, since they are the ones who often hold the keys to whether they'll allow you and your organization access, we thought you might like to know how *they* see it.

*In summary, a **Gumby** is all right for starters. But **one, two** or **three** **TEETH** in your value proposition(s) will help your organization's producers cut through the noise and confusion, to the senior executive levels you may desire, at a faster pace.*

All Packaged Up With a Gold Bow

The key point here is—your organization should strive to attain a level where your value propositions are *so clear*, *concise*, and *specific* to the audiences you desire—that they are like a *beautifully wrapped gift* with red foil paper and a shiny gold bow—begging to be tugged at, so that the package falls open with one gentle tug. And the audience(s) you are targeting know exactly what *it* is, and how *it* will help them.

Remember, in one sense, you are presenting them with a gift. *The gift of your offerings' value for their organization*. Therefore, make *sure* it is worth giving.

CHAPTER SEVEN
Try Building Yourself a New and Improved One

A well-articulated value proposition is worth millions of dollars in additional top-line revenue to any organization. And even if you feel you may need some work in this area, *especially if you market several product, service, or solution offerings to different vertical industry sectors*—we will provide some guidelines to help you think about what your value propositions *should* communicate. The following checklist provides a proven framework to help your organization begin down that path.

Laying a Cement Foundation

Anyone or any organization interested in building a solid value proposition that will *work* and *endure* needs to build upon a solid foundation like cement. So in building up to the climax of your true value to another organization, it is smart to begin on the ground floor by assessing, reassessing, then defining the net benefits of your products, services, and solutions.

There are really *two parts* to this process, if you wish to make things easier on your prospect or client. There are the net benefits of a *particular product or service*, and the net benefits of *doing business with your organization*.

There are companies so tunnel-focused on the net benefits of a particular product or service, that they often don't know how to articulate the net benefits of working with them *as an organization*. This is as critical as the first part. We will coach you to do both, if you want to do it most effectively, in a manner that clients appreciate. Let's begin by focusing on the net benefits of your organization's or business unit's product, service or solution.

Crystallize the Net Benefits of Your Offer

Part of your job as a professional, respectful influencer is to communicate to each prospect or client the key net benefits that your product, service or solution can deliver to their organization. And because they are always crunched for time, and have their own *opinions* as to what they do and do not need, you've got to communicate these net benefits quickly and clearly, so they're easy to remember.

In the space provided, we urge you to fill out—product by product, service by service, or solution by solution, what you believe to be your most powerful—honest—and compelling *core* net benefits for each product, service or solution you wish to address. Here is one tip before you begin.

In our consulting work with clients we have noticed that sometimes the product or service marketing teams don't communicate all that well with the sales organization(s)—and vice versa. And its the sales organization that usually gets to communicate the net benefits *cooked up* by the marketing department(s), so that they can ultimately sell something.

Both groups have great insight and experience regarding how to define and communicate the core net benefits. The problem is, these groups rarely get the chance to work together and share their knowledge—consequently they are not synergized. Instead, they are kept in separate *camps* by their organization. *"The marketing department says that these four things are our net benefits, so—go out and sell the stuff!"*

Our recommendation is to put these groups together physically, or at least by phone, video conference or web cast, so there is greater mind-sharing, and a much better chance for genuine buy-in across the marketing, sales and business development organization(s). If you do this, your organization will come up with *tighter* net benefits, and there will be less finger pointing.

In a nutshell, begin by listing the product, service or capabilities you wish to address, then define the core three or four *net* benefits of that product, service, solution or capability. We've provided five different product/service/capabilities for you to review. If you have more, keep the exercise going on another sheet of paper or flip chart. Remember, these net benefits should be honest, provable, measurable, and directly related to the general or specific needs, goals and objectives of your prospect or client organization(s).

Name of Product or Service: _____

    Net Benefit: _____

    Net Benefit: _____

    Net Benefit: _____

Name of Product or Service: _____

    Net Benefit: _____

    Net Benefit: _____

    Net Benefit: _____

Name of Product or Service: _____

    Net Benefit: _____

    Net Benefit: _____

    Net Benefit: _____

Name of Product or Service: _____

    Net Benefit: _____

    Net Benefit: _____

    Net Benefit: _____

Name of Product or Service: _____

    Net Benefit: _____

    Net Benefit: _____

    Net Benefit: _____

After you have defined the net benefits of your core products and services, you must now do *part two*, because it will make things easier on your prospect and client. You must now define *the net benefits of doing business with your organization.* Seriously—this is very important, and hard to do because there will be different opinions within your organization as to what the *real* net benefits are. We recommend bringing together some of your senior management, marketing folks, the sales management and producers. They will all have pretty good feedback, which will need to be channeled properly to help you get to the core answers to these questions: *"Just exactly why should other companies do business with us. From an organization standpoint—not from a product, service, or suite of offerings standpoint—what are the core net benefits that we as an organization deliver or bring to our clients?"* These are very tough questions to answer—but let the discussions begin.

The net benefits of doing business with your organization are:

1. _____

    _____

2. _____

    _____

3. _____

    _____

4. _____

    _____

Keep them crisp and accurate. Then share them with the rest of your organization for feedback, and shape according to where you receive the strongest internal buy-in. It's pretty hard to fool your own people, so select those net benefits that truly resonate with your own troops—especially with your front-line producers.

Nail Down Your Key Points of Difference

Net benefits are an important first step in building toward a well-crafted, articulate and solidly-anchored corporate, or product, service, or solution-oriented value proposition. However, you must not stop here because your work is just starting to get interesting.

Because things have become more complex and *gray* in many cases, and because most prospects and clients are pretty wise shoppers, key net benefits are fine—but in relationship to what—or whom? Prospective buyers are always pushing you toward the next natural step in the progression of their decision making process, which is, *"That's nice—so you have some net benefits. They sound good. So how do they stack up against these other product and service options I'm also considering?"*

You know that few business people nowadays only look at one option. It's more like *one* plus *three, four,* or *five* other comparable alternatives. Since this is almost always the case regardless of the business you are in, why allow the client to drag you and your producers there by default?

Lead them into this next step of their deciphering process by having already thought through—crystallized—condensed and articulated via proper *word-smithing*—your key points of difference in relationship to the other competitive, or *perceived to be* comparable product or service alternatives you *anticipate* you will be compared against. Those who have done a good job of clearly articulating their key points of difference in relationship to the other competitive offerings available, will go a long way toward earning credibility with the prospect or client.

Why? Because *if* they are clear, well-articulated and easily understood—it will help *cut the wheat from the chaff* faster. It also takes the hassle and frustration out of what can often be a confusing process. Remember, there are usually three to five good alternatives for almost every product, service or solution on the planet.

Before we offer you some suggestions to help you define your key points of difference—here is an analogy to drive home this point.

I enjoy cars. Even though I've been a four-wheel drive, SUV-man for the past several years, I recently looked at the new Audi A8 Quattro, the Volvo four-door sedan, the BMW 5 and 7 series, the Lexus and Acura sedans, and the Mercedes S Class 400 series.

As you car enthusiasts know, the Acura and Volvo are similar in price. The rest get kind of spendy. Here's the point. As I walked into the Audi dealership, circled the A8 on the show floor, opened the door and sat in the driver's seat, up popped a well-dressed man asking if I had any questions he could answer. Since I had already done some homework on the vehicle before showing up, and because I already knew some of the *key features and net benefits*, I jumped ahead to a question about the *key points of difference* between the Audi A8 and the Lexus, BMW, and Mercedes. *"How does the A8 compare to the Lexus, BMW 5 series, and the Mercedes 400 series in regard to resale value, horse power, ride, and amount of room in the backseat?"* The guy looked at me like I was some kind of freak. He paused, was silent for a moment, then said, "What—are you with Car and Driver, or Motortrend Magazine or something?" *"No"* I said, *"I'm sincerely interested in the car, and I'm comparing it to the others I mentioned. So what are the key differences that I would notice?"*

His answer was disappointing. *"You know—good question—but I don't really know the answer to that. I only sell Audis—not BMWs, Lexus, or Mercedes—so I guess you'll have to go drive them to find out. I'm sorry. Would you like a brochure on the car?"*

Now I'm not making fun of the salesman—the dealership—or Audi, the manufacturer. What I am attempting to point out is, *had he known the answers*, I would have stayed engaged, and in the dealership for a longer period of time. And who knows where the conversation would have lead. Instead, I left with a brochure—never drove the car—and never returned or called the guy again. Hence, I didn't buy the car, perhaps because he wasn't *helping me*—by crystallizing in my mind, the key points of difference between the products of interest to me.

You can do this exercise with any product, service or solution you desire.

To assist you in nailing down your key points of difference, compile the knowledge you have inside your organization on the five most direct competitors you have—or bump into the most. From this collateral, product and service literature, or annual reports, begin to dissect this information to get at what your competitors are saying their net benefits are, for each product or service they market. Also, try to understand what each competitor is saying, are *the net benefits of doing business with their organization.*

Once you've done this, compare. Line up your product or service net benefits against each competitive offering, then stare at them until you can begin to articulate where the key points of difference are—if there are any. To make it easier, you can fill out the matrix provided on the next page. We suggest doing this for each product, service, solution, or capabilities set you wish to analyze.

As you go through this process, try not to get so wound up that you begin *making things up*. Your key points of difference should be honest, provable, and articulate. The clearer they are, the more you help your prospect or client decipher from the various selections on their plate. And until you've sat on the other side— on a large task force chartered to analyze their organization's needs and requirements, then build a specification for those requirements, write an RFP (request for proposal), submit it to potential vendors, then read through the responses to try to figure out "what-is-what"—you have no idea how confusing it can be, to make sense of five different vendors all coming at you at once—saying they can help you. Therefore, those who do their homework, and do a clear job of defining their key points of difference, will go much further toward closing the business. That has been our experience, and it bears out with clients.

Competitive Offering: _____

Net Benefit: _____

Net Benefit: _____

Net Benefit: _____

Competitive Offering: _____

Net Benefit: _____

Net Benefit: _____

Net Benefit: _____

Competitive Offering: _____

Net Benefit: _____

Net Benefit: _____

Net Benefit: _____

Competitive Offering: _____

Net Benefit: _____

Net Benefit: _____

Net Benefit: _____

As you compare—Your Key Points of Difference, for this product/service are:

Key Point of Difference #1: _____

Key Point of Difference #2: _____

Key Point of Difference #3: _____

One additional suggestion as you complete this exercise. *Take the focus off of you, your offerings, and what you want.* Instead, *put on the face, mind, and heart of your prospect and client.* This is the audience to whom you will be presenting your value propositions. And as you know, their impressions and opinions of your net benefits and key points of difference matter. It is the only vote that counts.

Remember, there is a *part two* for this exercise as well. As we mentioned earlier, it's now time to make the same comparison of:

—*The net benefits of doing business with your organization, in comparison to,*
—*What your direct competitors say are the net benefits of doing business with them—as an organization.*

Again, we suggest you chart this out so you and your team members can see where your key points of difference lie, in regard to doing business with your organization. This is very important if you want to paint the full picture for prospects and clients.

This process helps drive your organization to find your own *value equation.* It can help you learn where the financial value is for each of your offerings.

The visual of what you are doing looks like this:

The net benefits of your product/service/solution are:

_____

_____

_____

The net benefits of doing business with your organization are:

_____

_____

_____

The key points of difference of your product/service/solution are:

_____

_____

_____

The key points of difference (in relationship to these "x" competitors) of doing business with your organization are:

_____

_____

_____

Therefore, your Generic Value Propositions are:

1. _____

2. _____

3. _____

And your Custom Shaped Value Propositions are:

1. _____

2. _____

3. _____

Broad-Brush Value Proposition Category Options
for Starters

The percentage of market share, level of quality, service and support, size of annual research and development expenditure, lowest total cost of ownership, percentage of up-time/reliability, quality of migration path, overall performance, best in class, and best of breed are a few value proposition category options for starters.

After you have finished defining *your net benefits and key points of difference*, around your core products and services—and around you as an organization, you are now ready to select the categories where you believe your real value to another organization rests.

These categories *all* sound impressive, but selecting those that best suit you and your offerings can be a seductive trap. Why? Because you must be able to explain the answers to the questions, *"In relationship to what—or whom?"* And again, many business professionals can't. Here is a story that illustrates this point.

The cover story on *Business Week* Magazine's March 5, 2001 European edition was entitled, *"Downfall—The Inside Story of the Management Fiasco at Xerox."* It explains that once Richard Thoman had been installed as the new CEO, one of the first things he did was order a review of the economics of the existing Xerox product line. He was presented with charts showing that Xerox was "world class" in terms of manufacturing and development costs. (Perhaps this was also part of the sales pitch the sales organization was using, even though there is no proof this was the case.)

After hearing "world class" more than a few times, Mr. Thoman's response to his own people was, *"How do you know? They told me they'd get back to me."* The third time he got this answer, he put his foot down. It turned out that staffers had relied on a sampling of 1994 market data so limited as to exclude most of Xerox's Japanese competitors. Thoman ordered them back to the drawing board. Weeks later, he was finally presented evidence that Xerox had failed to maintain its hard-won parity with the Japanese.

So many business professionals *throw around language* like "world class", "best of breed", "low cost provider", etc. Yet to some senior officers, they *still* view some of these terms as *"hot air"*. Often, the people using these terms use them when they shouldn't. They're usually not prepared to back up their glowing statements, because they don't know how.

To drive this point home a bit further, I was recently facilitating a *corporate value proposition workshop* for a broadband/ telecommunications client, when one of their senior marketing people blurted out: *"We've got best in class voice over IP (internet protocol) and mobility solutions!"* We said, "Great—what does that mean really—and in relationship to whom?" Without replaying the entire session, let's just say the answer took a long time to get to. We call this *uncovering the fluff*. Even though this organization had an impressive track record, and a respectable list of satisfied clients, they had difficulty in justifying the language their sales and senior executives were using. Helping them drill-down to the answers that backed up their claims was a rewarding exercise, which is now helping them close more business.

If you plan to use *trendy* language to describe your offerings' value, such as "best in class" or "best of breed", be able to explain what that really means. Otherwise, you leave you and your producers exposed.

Therefore, don't fall in love with any one of these value proposition categories as such. They are just categories—that's all. The key will always be to find the core answers to: *"That's nice—so what does that mean—really?"* In the examples provided, both parties had a hard time answering that question. We suggest you use phrases or categories you can explain and justify with *TEETH* —and avoid the fluff.

Define Specifically What You Need it, and Want it To do for You

What if—as an organization or business unit, you decided to calibrate your value propositions to *reduce your own selling cycles?* How could you do this? One way would be to identify the titles of the executives who could help you *drive* your sales process to closure faster, in a top-down fashion, if they were impressed with your message. If you like this idea, determine who those executives are, then identify *exactly* what you need to have happen in meeting number one. Then begin to tailor your value propositions to appeal to those executives, to achieve your desired result.

Back Into Your Action Steps With Baby Steps— Exactly Backwards

Exactly backwards means this. Many companies, entrepreneurs, senior executives, and sales professionals *allow* their prospect or client to determine *what should happen next* in all meetings and interactions.

However, there is a smarter way. Revisit the grid in Chapter Two, page 20, called *Block and Tackle Out Your Current Sales Process*. Analyze your answers and think through how you could shorten your own sales cycles.

What would need to happen in your process in order to strip one, two, three, or four meetings or interactions out of your cycle? This is precisely what we have been able to achieve for our clients, collapsing their sales and closing cycles.

Once you come up with some new ideas on how to do this within your organization, try this idea on for size. What if you simply decided the following: *"We are now going to run our standard sales process in "x" many meetings, and we will attempt to adhere to this new standard as best we can."* Some will say you can't do this, and others will say why not?

If you choose to try it, you will get some resistance from some of your producers, perhaps even senior management, who may say, *"Are you nuts? We can't tell the prospect or client how they are going to work with us. It depends on what they want and need, not what we want. It's not about us—it's about them."*

Well—now wait a minute. Let me offer another side to this picture. Let's look through the *smoke*, and perhaps some fear. Don't most people tend to respect—even admire others who know *exactly* what they want, and then go after it? People who say, *"Here's what we're going to do"*, or *"Here's how this is going to work."* You would probably say yes, as long as they go about things in an honorable, ethical and non-offensive manner.

Therefore, we challenge you and your organization to consider redesigning how you'd like your new sales and business development processes to work and flow.

Chunk it out backwards. How many meetings or interactions would you like before you are able to close and sign a piece of business? If the answer is five, keep moving forward. Figure out exactly what needs to happen in meetings number five, then four, three, two, and one. We call this thought process *"backing into your action steps with baby steps—exactly backwards."*

This will take some thinking, group discussion, debate, and possibly some good old-fashioned arguing to work things out to everyone's satisfaction, but it's all for the continued success of your business.

Who Are You Trying to Talk to?
—Levels and Titles Please

If you haven't already done this exercise in Chapter Five, pages 39-41, we hope you will. We urge you to involve your sales and business development professionals, and their upline management. The rationale for this is, if you don't come to some type of understanding and agreement, it can be difficult to gain any kind of passionate, meaningful, or lasting buy-in from the sales organization—the people charged with finding and closing additional business.

Do You Need Two or More Value Propositions?

Perhaps. It depends on how many product, service, or solution offerings you're attempting to condense down, inside each business unit of your organization.

We have worked with multi-national corporations with forty plus different product, service, and solution offerings, and condensed their key offerings into three or four articulate, financially calibrated bullet point statements that speak volumes to the targeted audiences the client desired.

Based on our experience with clients, mid-sized and larger organizations sometimes need different, custom value propositions for each vertical industry sector in which they operate, and custom value propositions for the suite of offerings underneath each business unit. They also need value propositions for new product, service and solution launches. Sometimes, specific value propositions designed to explain a recent company merger, acquisition, downsizing, or legal event are also necessary, based on the desired result. Suffice it to say—start with one or two, and see if they capsulize the core essence of what all of your offerings really produce, or deliver for your clients.

Align it to the Levels of Decision Makers Who Really Make The Call—Not the Ones Who Say They Can, But Can't or Won't, Without a Congressional Mandate

You've probably done this in the earlier chapters, however if you haven't, please do (Chapter Five, page 41, questions A, B and C). Be honest with yourself, your senior management team, and the sales organization as you answer these questions.

The sales and business development organization should be excited about your new value propositions. They should also understand the necessity for why these messages contain the *wordsmithed* language that they do. This is why clients send their producers through *The Circle of Leverage® System Basic and Advanced Training™ Programs*, where they receive the education and the understanding about why their value propositions need to be calibrated, typically to vice president levels and above.

As mentioned earlier, many mid to lower level managers don't really care, or understand the beauty of a good, articulate value proposition. But don't sweat the small stuff. If you want to collapse your sales process, aim higher with your value propositions, if they are really sharp.

In summary, ask yourself this question. Whom do you want deciding your and your company's fate as to whether you win a piece of business? Five, ten or fifteen people on a task force who don't really care about a well-defined value proposition? Or a couple senior vice presidents who operate at 50,000 feet, and have the power, authority, and self-confidence to make the decision quickly—if they are impressed with your offerings? Whom would you prefer? I know who I'd choose.

Give It Some Shiny New *TEETH*

What are *TEETH*? *TEETH* are the financial metrics mentioned earlier in Chapter Six, pages 43-48. Based on 20 years of street experience in selling complex, large scale solutions to senior executive levels of Fortune 1000 companies:

*If there are no **TEETH**—no financial metrics in your value propositions, you can have a great sounding bunch of words or catchy "marketing speak", and they still won't give you the "pop"—the "lift"—or the attention you are hoping to garner from a senior level audience. It is that important!*

***TEETH** are **mandatory** in your value propositions—if gaining access and more exposure to senior executive levels is a necessary requirement for how you want your new sales process to work and flow.*

Why? Because *money* is what's on their minds—at least for the majority. They are concerned with driving the stock price up, reducing debt levels, improving margins and profits, becoming more nimble, stream-lined—doing things faster, and maybe even better. Dumping non-core businesses. Amassing more cash for a potential acquisition. Reducing the legal exposure or the amount of litigation. Increasing market share. Beating the competition to market with a new product, service, or solution, etc.

*So, if your value propositions **do** contain financial metrics that can be backed-up, measured, verified, or benchmarked, you can increase your ability of being heard by senior executive level decision makers—for a while, until your claims are explained, verified, or substantiated. We'll get to this shortly in the next section.*

Can we provide examples of what we've been talking about? Yes. We have delivered effective work on behalf of our clients, in regards to creating and articulating the financial metrics inside their value propositions. Work that has earned them additional top-line revenues.

The question really becomes, is this the proper forum—a business book—in which to provide some examples? Well I will in Chapter Ten—provide a few case histories, and some real life examples.

Remember however, there are several variables that go into the design, calibration, and word-smithing of a client's value proposition. No two are alike. Each statement is carefully designed around the specific goals, objectives, products, services, and solutions of the client—calibrated to the levels of access they desire in meeting number one. They are also designed to address the competitive situation of the moment, and whether the opportunity is with a new prospect or an existing client. Please keep these things in mind as you read the examples and case histories provided in Chapter Ten.

If we were to provide this service for your organization, we'd need to understand all of the above elements so that we could do an effective job.

One last thought. Analyzing, calibrating, and word-smithing the financial metrics—**the TEETH**, that go inside a client's value proposition(s), can be one of the toughest, most challenging parts of the entire process. It is what many clients wrestle with, which is why some request assistance. It is not an area in which "shooting from the hip" is a good idea.

Back it Up. Everybody's Skeptical—Some Afraid

Once you have attempted putting some *TEETH* in your value proposition(s), we now come to another important topic of discussion, and that is **fear**. Fear of change, fear of uncertainty, fear of being *afraid* for goodness sakes.

This topic is a hot button. The recent lack of leadership in Corporate America—the *casualness*—the *lack of courtesy* and *respect* displayed toward customers—the *laziness* that is allowed to exist in some companies, and the amazing willingness that some have for doing things "half-baked", even though they know their decision or indecision, will come back to bite them and their employer in the behind at some later date.

These are very real issues, which may get worse before they get better. It's frustrating when people with a fairly simple decision to make can't seem to make one, but would rather get *10 other people* involved in the process, or kick the decision *upstairs* for a final decision, so it's out of their hands.

The facts are that most people are not leaders, they prefer to follow because it's a safer option. You already know this, and the mere fact that you have picked up this book, already proves that you're "out-front". You *are* a leader, or you wouldn't be investing your time in this subject matter. However, many folks are fearful of making a basic recommendation, unless there are five to 10 others who agree with the same recommendation. Few people nowadays want to *stand up and be counted*. They would rather blend in, just in case things go *sideways*. That way, they can't be targeted or blamed for a decision gone awry. Why then mention the obvious?

Because when you and your producers appear on the scene attempting to gain access, the clearer you are with the financial metrics, the more you *infer* that you are able to backup and substantiate the claims in your value propositions.

This is important for many reasons. Some of us can, at times, be pretty skeptical, jaded, and full of sarcasm toward anyone attempting access to us. Plus, everyone's had a few *difficult* experiences where they've been fooled or taken advantage of. Therefore, when someone comes along and says, *"Here's how we can help you"*, then gets even more specific by providing percentages, ranges, time-frames, specific increases or decreases, etc., the impression put forth is that *you've done this before* somewhere else.

This draws more prospects and clients to you and your organization, because it *appears* that you've got some substance to your message, especially when you're able to back-up your claims. Therefore, be ready to—or don't make the claims.

There are several ways to validate the claims in your value propositions. What about some type of *condensed financial analysis or comparison?* This is another area where we've added value for clients, helping them create the framework they use to validate their value propositions.

This concept is *key* to collapsing your selling and closing cycles because it allows those individuals who may be reluctant to "stick their neck out", or support your product, service, or solution—to have an easier time doing so.

The Generic Capabilities Value Proposition

Most of us can improve in the area of becoming better communicators. There's always a few who think that every time they speak, the golden gates of heaven open up, and they're given exactly what they want, but most of us can get better.

If you took your own message or value proposition(s) as they stand right now, would you rate yours as *kind-of-loose* or *tough to substantiate*? If you're being candid, you might even say they're a little *gray*. Maybe they are this way on purpose, so you have some room to negotiate with prospects and clients. However, consider this statement again:

"If you do business with us...we can help you by:

1. _____
   _____
   _____

2. _____
   _____
   _____

3. _____
   _____
   _____.*"

If and when you are able to be *this specific* with your desired target audiences, not only will they appreciate how precise you are, but most will respond like this:

"Wow—this is unbelievable—someone we can understand. These people are actually clear. We need to meet with this company!"

This should become a goal for your enterprise to work toward. You might call it your *elevator speech*, but it's more than that. Besides, if you analyze your elevator speech, is it that *tight*? Perhaps there's some room for further *buttoning-up*.

The Generic Capabilities Value Proposition is again, generic and general. *It is not product, service, or solution specific,* per say. Many senior level executives will admit that they really don't care too much about the specifics of an organization's product, service, or solution. They don't want to get *that granular*. In fact, many believe *they don't need to know the details*—others within their organization will validate that stuff. Instead, they want to know *how* and *why* all of what you bring to the table, can impact and benefit them—again in financial terms, if you can.

Therefore we challenge you to roll up your sleeves and go to work. Drill-down to the real financial value that your organization's specific offerings bring to the table, as we've mentioned in earlier chapters. Start defining the statements that could *generically* play in the vertical industry sectors in which you do business—explaining how you could financially impact their business. *This is the Generic Capabilities Value Proposition.*

The Custom Shaped Value Proposition— Focused to the Prospect or Customer's Self-Stated Goals, Objectives and Challenges

For maximum impact, your value propositions should include the *Generic* and the *Custom Shaped*. The *Generic* ones communicate the core ways in which you can generally impact the prospect or client. The *Custom Shaped* value propositions go one step further, by linking and explaining how your generic claims will help them solve a specific, self-stated goal, objective, or challenge, as mentioned in their annual report, or the information you've sourced.

By linking your statements to how you could impact very specific goals or objectives they wish to address—you become viewed as a trusted advisor, someone who has done their homework, and is therefore more credible and worthy of their time.

As you walk through this thought process, be as objective as you can be. For those with a more dictatorial personality—keep your tempers in check if this process becomes frustrating. No one likes sharing his/her own thoughts or ideas with a *hot-head* who doesn't welcome input.

This exercise can be complex—a mental chess game, but it is directly connected to the continued success of your business going forward.

CHAPTER EIGHT
Take It Out for a Hard Spin

"No senior executive—no matter how large the organization—how prestigious their title—or what their compensation package may be—no senior executive is 'above' presenting their new value propositions to the audiences who really hold the ultimate vote, the prospective customer or existing client."

Present It to the Real Message Carriers—
Your Sales People. Did They Laugh, Applaud,
or Roll their Eyes?

Once you finish tweaking your new value propositions, the first and most natural audience in which to *try them on for size* is your own sales producers. Since they are the ones living on the street, going toe-to-toe with prospects and clients on a daily basis—they are usually a pretty good gauge as to what will *play* in the field, and what will not. Therefore, we recommend presenting them with some fanfare—excitement—and pizzazz. Then sit back, *watch* and *listen*.

Watch for the non-verbals they give you. Listen for initial gut reactions and comments. This feedback is important. If you *package* the exchange so they know and trust that their comments won't come back around to bite them in the behind—you should get some fairly open and honest feedback.

If they fire comments, suggestions, and opinions in an honest effort to improve upon what has been presented, *avoid* becoming defensive or guarded. Try to understand the reasoning behind their comments so they are not lost. Often, their initial reactions are important to hear and heed because they are the *mirror* for how the prospective customer or client will respond.

Therefore, when presenting these shiny new value propositions to the real message carriers, you should be hoping for cheers, smiles, maybe even some applause, even though it's much *cooler* and more corporate nowadays to remain *tempered* with a look of *concern*.

If you *don't* hear much, or if you see people rolling their eyes, that's usually a bad sign indicating they're not sold or convinced. In this case, you've got more work to do. I've always believed that if you can *sell a sales force* on your value propositions—meaning they truly understand, believe, and are genuinely excited to go share them—you've probably done a good job.

Let me share a quick story about a company we recently witnessed, presenting their new value propositions to their global sales organization of about 350 producers, at their annual convention.

A while back, Dr. Ken Blanchard, (Co-author of the international best-selling business book *The One Minute Manager*, and one of the foremost business authors and speakers on the topic of organizational change within companies), and I were invited to provide general session keynote addresses at this company's annual meeting.

Just prior to our addresses, we were sitting in the audience of this large, publicly held, e-commerce and e-solutions company, as the President stood and presented to the entire organization, their *new corporate value proposition.*

So *boom—there they were*—on two huge IMAX-type screens for everyone to see, as he read them aloud to the audience, explaining the logic and rationale behind how the senior management team had come up with these marvelous works of wisdom, which, by the way were vague, unmetriced, soft and "gray".

I'm not exaggerating—you could have heard a pin drop, even though the ballroom was carpeted. It was painful. There was total silence. No one said anything. *No one.* Just blank stares from the audience. We watched it all unfold, and were embarrassed for the President of this organization.

In fact, he *felt* the lack of buy-in, and started to ramble, hoping to engage the audience with at least a few questions. And yes, a few questions did come. But the key point here is—the sales organization—the people who had to carry the message forward were totally *uninspired and unimpressed.* Some began to whisper to each other, *"Man, they don't get it. This won't fly. It doesn't say anything. What the heck am I supposed to do with this?"*

This type of situation happens frequently, therefore, this organization is certainly not alone. Worst of all, the *senior management* of this organization—even after receiving a less than luke-warm response—*still* thought they had *nailed* the message. Based on the sales organization's reaction, they couldn't have been farther off the mark.

Passionate buy-in from your producers is a *must* before ever presenting these messages to your target audiences. Therefore, work toward attaining it.

Hit the Street—Present it Yourself

We probably agree that it's not a good idea to micro-manage sales producers. However, it is important that you learn for yourself how your target audiences respond to your new value propositions. See their faces and reactions. Hear their comments and responses. There is nothing better than *direct* feedback.

Go with your producers and present these new messages yourself. You'll receive direct feedback you can learn from, and you send an important message to your people that says, *"Wow—this really is important if the Vice President is presenting our new value proposition."* In the end, you will win both ways.

Torque According to What Works— Not the Board of Directors' Opinions

For those who attended college, remember those professors who sounded so wise, all-knowing and competent *in the classroom*? It is one thing to philosophize about how things *should* work in the business world, quite another to learn that some of those philosophies don't work too well—outside of the classroom.

If what's *cooked up* in the classroom doesn't *play* in the real world of business, then who's right; the professors, or the people on the street who have to shape, mold, and tweak the theories learned in the classroom, to make them work in the real world?

And so it is with the individuals who comprise your organization's Board of Directors. Yes, they are important people. They are all very capable, or they would not have been invited to sit on the board. However, being on the board is a long way from the "street". Hence, it's easier for them to *play professor* with your value propositions. Remember, *they* are typically not the ones who have to *present* and *sell* these messages and value propositions. It's the producers who have to do that.

Therefore, we recommend you torque your messages according to what you find works on the street versus trying to appease your board members. Certainly it's important to appease the board, but *if your value propositions don't work on the street—__you__ will be the one looking for a new position faster than anyone on the board*!

Beware of *The Marketing "Experts"*

Here are a few more observations we've learned from working with our clients.

— Some marketing executives have never sold anything. They have rarely been on the street, banging on doors trying to get an appointment at senior executive levels, then articulating to the correct, but skeptical target audience, why they *might* be worth being listened to.

— A few marketing executives have a difficult time explaining concisely, *what* and *how* all of their offerings specifically benefit the client.

— A few marketing executives don't appreciate being challenged about their company's printed material/collateral, web site content and design, video or direct mail campaigns, or white papers.

— There are some marketing executives who focus much of their collateral around the product, service, or solution—the features and the benefits, versus the *real financial value* that the offerings provide.

— Sometimes there is an attitude (or a lack of respect) coming from the marketing department toward the sales and business development organization, that they are a necessary evil *one just has to deal with.*

— Many marketing executives seem to believe that providing *more* information to the prospect or client about their organization's products or services, is much better than providing less.

The philosophy seems to be, *"Let's educate the customer—let's help them, by giving them **all** of the information they ask for, at whatever time in the sales process they ask for it. I mean—let's make it easy for them to buy—not hard. Therefore, **more** must be better, because it helps them."*

These are merely observations we've experienced in hopes it will shed some light, and ultimately be helpful.

We have shaped and *word-smithed* several clear, crisp, and "plain-languaged" value propositions on behalf of our clients, only to submit them for approval—then find some of them reworked, re-languaged and *totally watered down* so that it was *very difficult*—if not impossible to understand quickly, why anyone would want to sit with one of the company's sales representatives.

When this happens, the value propositions come back to us so beautifully worded with "fancy" language, that they often sound like *mush*. However, *most CEO's nowadays want the opposite.* They want *short, fast, clear, plain-languaged, common-sense based, non-fluff oriented bullet points.* That is what they want. We hear this frequently.

Something else we hear from the sales and business development organizations is that their own marketing department produces and distributes *so much information* about what they are selling, that it actually works against them, making it much harder to get a face-to-face meeting with the prospect or existing client.

The producers usually say, *"the prospects and existing clients are telling us that they're getting all of their initial questions answered from our website, our collateral, CD's and brochures, and that there's really no need—no reason to meet. So how are we supposed to make our numbers when we can't even get in front of them?"*

There are solutions to these issues that have to do with how you shape your value propositions.

When you shape your value propositions, we recommend that the President/CEO/Owner, EVP, SVP, and VP of business development or strategic growth, marketing, finance, perhaps customer service, and a few key sales managers and producers from each region be present. Why? Because it's typically the sales producers on the street who temper the top executives' *theories* and *philosophies* about what *should* play—with what actually *will* play in the field.

When you only involve *the marketing "experts"* in the creation of your value propositions without any "street" representation, you will end up with marketing language so *smooth, eloquent, and "vanilla"*, that you may not sell much!

Nail it Down Smooth

Rarely does anyone nail things on the first attempt. It usually takes some finessing and tweaking. And so it is with your value propositions.

You really won't know too much until you present your new value propositions to the audiences who have the final vote, the prospect or client. If you appreciate feedback and actually get some, most organizations find they need more tweaking in order to make them work correctly. Therefore, you shouldn't expect anything different, unless you get lucky right out of the gate.

Solicit feedback from prospects and clients until you find them saying something like, *"You know—your message was so clear and easy to understand, we knew exactly how your organization could help us, and we knew we needed to visit with your firm."*

Strive for that and you will have *nailed it down smooth*.

CHAPTER NINE
Brush Daily for a Consistent Shine

Keeping your *TEETH* healthy and looking their best takes a concerted effort, one that requires constant attention. If you want good results from your new value propositions, it's important that you do the same.

It's a good idea to revisit your value propositions *every ninety days* as things in your organization change, like new product and service offerings, company acquisitions, competitive offerings, etc. This way they'll remain current, and as on-point as they can be—calibrated of course, to the levels of executives of whom you desire more attention. Therefore, a *value proposition check-up* every ninety days is advised.

Cascade Your Value Propositions Throughout All Mediums and Touch Points, to Prevent Cavities and Decay

Once you pass your *ninety day value proposition exam* and are comfortable that yours are relevant and on-point, it's now time to discuss what you'd like to do with them. Our question is this: "Are you and your producers the only people you want carrying forward these new value propositions? Or would you consider using them in other mediums of communication such as direct mail, company collateral, your website, company letterhead, etc.—*constantly reminding* your target audiences of your core value propositions.

For those in a position to employ a marketing, public relations, or advertising agency to help "get your message out there", wouldn't it make sense to carry these same messages forward in a consistent manner? Wouldn't that make it even easier for those you're attempting to attract?

Once you are pleased with your value propositions, you've tested them on your target audiences, and they seem to resonate, what if you cascaded these messages throughout those additional mediums and *touch points*, where your people interact with existing customers and prospective clients?

Striving toward having everyone in your organization who touches a prospective or existing customer—be able to communicate your core value propositions, then if necessary, *walk the prospect or customer backwards*, through an explanation of your key points of difference, key net benefits of your product, service and solutions—in addition to those that your organization brings to the table, provides a level of consistency that will help prevent *cavities and decay* within your organization.

Cascading your value propositions throughout additional mediums can actually help you become a better steward of your prospects' and clients' time—making you and your offerings more worthy and valuable.

CHAPTER TEN
Sharp-Toothed Credibility Bricks

Everyone nowadays wants *hard data*, and backup data that substantiates the claims/statements in your value propositions. Because we have made some statements in this book, we thought we should back them up. You will then have some *proof* that the concepts set forth really work and deliver results.

Therefore, it's time to share a few examples of how clients are benefiting from these powerful and common sense oriented concepts.

In honoring our confidential relationships with clients, we cannot share the names of the organizations, but the situations are real. Secondly, we cannot share *all* of the specifics, but you *will* get some ***TEETH***.

Case Histories of Client Successes

<u>Success Number One</u>

The Organization: An information technology solutions firm with services including business innovation consulting, digital strategy, e-solutions, customer relationship management and application development maintenance outsourcing. Annual revenues exceed $700 million dollars.

The Premise/Problem/Challenge: Intense competition from a handful of global companies several times their revenue, with additional competition from smaller, regional-type players.

The Situation: There weren't any "panic"situations at the time, however, senior management knew the great run they were enjoying from Y2K related issues would begin to slow, and they'd need to focus on continuing to grow their revenue streams. Then hopefully projections would be met, Wall Street would "be nice", and everyone would be happy.

The Consequence if Left Untouched: The organization was doing well. However, as they continued to acquire smaller regional firms, the number of products, services, solutions, and capabilities kept expanding. Eventually, the sales organization had over forty different offerings to understand, explain, and hopefully sell. Hence *confusion* expanded. The producers, in order to hit their numbers, began focusing on all "the stuff" they could sell versus focusing on the financial business benefits— the real value these offerings could bring to the customer. However, there was difficulty in articulating the value equation.

Furthermore, the producers didn't know what to *lead* with. They were used to getting in at relatively low levels inside the IT organization, learning what the challenges were, so they could speak to whichever of the forty-plus offerings that were most pertinent for the client. However, the meetings and discussions were typically with lower level individuals, usually centered around *the minutia*— the bits, bites, features and benefits.

As the sales process progressed and higher levels of access were *slowly* granted, the producers had a hard time shifting the conversation onto the financial value their offerings could deliver. Hence, access to higher-ups was infrequent, and the sales cycles were beginning to drag.

It was *the chicken or the egg*. The producers would request higher levels of access—15 to 30 minutes—so they could listen, learn and understand the customer's *issues,* so they would know which product or service offering to lead with. But executives kept putting up barriers by saying, in effect:

*"Well before we decide if we'll sit with you, tell me how you can help us. What's the core idea? What's the net-net? What's the value proposition? Why do **I** need to be involved at this stage?"*

The producer's response was typically: *"Well, I don't know yet. That's a good question. I won't really know specifically how we can help, and what product, service, or solution might be appropriate for you, until we have the chance to sit down with you, or talk with you more about what your current goals, objectives and requirements are. So once we can do that—then I'll understand more about what you may need, and we can then speak to those issues with the proper offerings."*

This answer wasn't good enough for the vice presidents and other senior level executives. They were not willing to *sit and explain* first. They wanted a concisely wound statement that could explain the "net-net" first, so that if they liked the answer—they would *then* decide if they wanted or needed to be involved.

Therefore the rift continued, as did the general frustration among the producers, that either access was a problem, or that they didn't know how to communicate the financial value around each of their offerings to the higher-ups. They also had questions about how to approach a prospective or existing client opportunity until they were able *to get in first*—do the learning, listening, and qualifying, so they knew which offerings to focus on.

The challenge seemed to be they couldn't answer, in financial metrics, a key question being asked by the senior executives, which was: *"If I engage with your organization, what do we get, or what can you really do for us?"* Instead, their answer was: *"Well that's a good question. Let us come in and talk with you and we'll learn together where we can be of the most value. Don't forget, as a global provider, we have several happy clients in numerous vertical industry sectors."*

Again, to the core "D" or type "A" vice president, senior vice president or higher, this response usually didn't resonate. Hence, access to these levels early on in the process was more infrequent than the client desired.

The consequence lengthened the closing cycle, and there was an increase in the number of deals lost. There was also sincere frustration coming from the producers to "cool it" on acquiring more companies, and to create a message that might resonate more with senior executives. Couple these frustrations with the fact that revenues and margins needed to be there so that the analysts wouldn't downgrade the stock, and you have all the elements of a complex set of issues that needed to be addressed.

The Recommended Solution: We applied the concepts and methodologies in this book (along with others) with the senior management and sales organization. As a team, we condensed the communication of forty-plus offerings into three, well articulated, financially metriced statements that communicated what the real value, "lowsidehighside" could be, if the prospect or customer were to engage with our client. Each statement was calibrated to resonate with three to five senior people—the President/CEO, COO, CFO, and the most senior Information Technology Officer. It was also designed to resonate with specific business unit presidents and senior vice presidents.

It was *not* calibrated, nor probably appealing to lower levels within the information technology organization, but that was alright since that wasn't the client's target audience. According to the client, those individuals typically didn't have the *ultimate say so*, and they usually didn't sign the checks.

The Revised Approach: The value proposition created sounded something like this:

"If you do business with our organization, we can, through our capabilities, skill sets, experience, and over 40 different offerings, help you:

- *Strip between 5%- 15% out of the amount of money currently being spent annually on maintaining your existing legacy IT applications.*
- *Improve the quality of existing legacy IT applications service levels by 10% per year.*
- *Take this new found "chunk" of capital we have just "freed up", and re-deploy it, by helping you create, implement and manage your own e-commerce roadmap, giving you e-commerce solutions and customer facing IT processes that will help your business become leaner, faster, more flexible, and more profitable."*

"Said in plain English...without another dime spent on your total IT budget, we will "find"—within your existing IT annual budget, between _____ to _____ million dollars, and help you reinvest these dollars into e-commerce oriented solutions that will give you more control, so that you can drive your business to be leaner, faster, more flexible, and more profitable."

This is our value proposition to you and your organization.

The senior executives our client wanted to attract, didn't want to talk about the details, the specific features, bits and bites of *how* the solution would work. They had other people to benchmark and verify all of that stuff. They just wanted to focus on the *big picture stuff*, so we did. Their new value proposition was clear and financially oriented. It also encompassed several products, services, and solutions, even though we *led* with financially oriented statements.

As a result, the client was welcomed at more senior levels earlier on in their selling process more frequently, and with less resistance.

In addition, each statement was metriced to work with the others for the purpose of convincing the prospect or customer to allow our client to go through an exercise which we'll call *The Financial Comparison Model*. This allowed the client to financially benchmark and validate their claims in the value proposition early in their sales process, helping them keep their access to senior levels—which in turn helped drive the opportunities to closure more quickly.

This meant a *paradigm shift* for the sales producers in terms of what they were now selling. They now had new objectives to accomplish in meeting number one, which they welcomed. The focus now became *selling the need to validate the financial business case first*, versus focusing the message around the technology behind their solutions.

The Result: First, the producers are "staying out of the basement" of prospect and client IT departments more frequently by focusing on the financial value their offerings really drive.

Secondly, they are having more fun because their value propositions are more relevant and on-point to what is more important to the senior executive levels, giving them faster access. Therefore, they've been able to expand the scope of opportunities and close faster, which has translated into more commission dollars. This has been a positive benefit for management as well.

The new focus has also helped reinvigorate the senior management and the producers, because they feel as though their core message is clearer and easier to understand. They're having more fun presenting, which has translated into more enthusiastic presentations. This has positively impacted prospects and clients alike, who are also more excited, because now *they* can articulate the impact they would receive, back to their own senior management, which assists them is securing funding.

We will summarize with one last thought. The hard dollars realized as a result of this new focus has provided an ROI most pleasing to the client. Just one opportunity in particular proved to be several million dollars in additional revenue.

Success Number Two

The Organization: A consulting firm to the utilities industry, serving large scale utilities on a national and multi-national basis. Annual revenues were under $25 million at the time of our engagement.

The Premise/Problem/Challenge: There were not any major problems. The principals of the firm had a general desire to move their conversations up a notch or two, to executives inside these utilities who could hopefully make decisions faster. They believed this would help close business faster, expand the size and scope of the opportunities, and help them run a more efficient and profitable operation.

The Situation: There was no *compelling event* on their radar screen, just a genuine desire to operate more effectively and profitability.

The Consequence if Left Untouched: They were getting knocked out of deals they thought they were going to win, and it was becoming a bit irritating. They'd be going along just fine with a prospective opportunity, then out of left field, in would come a competitor, often at a higher level than they were, and wham—the deal was done. Over. Their contacts would shake their heads and apologize, saying they really didn't know what happened. It was the old: *"Gosh, I'm sorry guys. I really liked your process and methodology, and I was very comfortable with the potential of working with your organization, but I guess somebody in our home office had other ideas. However, I do want to keep in touch with you guys, just to stay abreast of what you're doing. I believe it's ground breaking stuff."* Since second prize wasn't putting dollars in the bank, our client was perturbed to put it mildly.

The Recommended Solution: A new value proposition that didn't focus on their process, methodology, capabilities or solutions. We worked with the principals to create very articulate language that spoke to a different audience than they were typically used to approaching or working with. The new language spoke to the CFO and VP of Finance, the Chief Operating Officer, and the business unit heads of specific divisions.

Our client was typically more comfortable with lower level management inside a prospective client, however they wanted to raise the level of discussion to people who could actually make a final decision, instead of a recommendation. Therefore, they *became* more open to learning how to present their message in 5-10 minutes, to a senior level audience, which we also helped them do.

We worked with their sales staff on how to apply *The COL™ System* in their business and industry, so that as we finished tweaking their value proposition, they would have a repeatable process to customize as needed, helping them gain access to more senior levels.

The Revised Approach: The language in their new value proposition will probably make no sense, unless you're in the utility industry, but it speaks volumes to the senior executives of the target utilities that were on the radar screen of our client. Notice when you read their value proposition, that it doesn't say too much about their products, services, or processes, but that's o.k. Remember who they were trying to attract.

"If you engage in a business relationship with our organization, we can help you—through our experience, capabilities, skill sets and specific processes, to:

- *Reduce your cost per mega watt hour, by 3.5% on the low side, by up to 6.5% on the high side.*
- *Increase your availability (your EAF) by the same range.*
- *Improve your reliability (your EFOR) by between 5% on the low side, by up to 20% on the high side, and,*
- *Reduce your operating costs (your O+M, non-fuel) in the range of between 2.5% to 10%.*

This is our value proposition to you and your organization, and why we are excited about the opportunity to help you achieve the above enhanced, financial and operational efficiencies."

Again, their value proposition was designed to engage senior executives who only wanted to discuss the *big picture stuff*. Thankfully, it did just that. Secondly, it drove the prospect toward agreeing to conduct an initial *financially oriented condensed comparison analysis* so our client could attain information from the prospect, to validate the claims in their value proposition.

Notice that each of the four statements allows a CFO or top financial executive to plug in their own numbers to see what the actual percentage increase or decrease would mean to them—a*ll before agreeing to meet with our client*. This is a *very* effective strategy.

The Result: Not only has our client enjoyed more senior levels of access, their value proposition is helping keep their prospects focused on the *financial* big picture first, until there is general "buy-in" on the core business drivers. Then—the prospect can focus on the more detailed intricacies of our client's "processes", with those mid-level people who still needed to make sure the solutions were valid, and would deliver on the claims stated in their value proposition.

Bottom line, the client continues to prosper, and the partners feel the objectives set forth, continue to be met.

One last note. Remember what we mentioned about putting *TEETH* in your value propositions—some sort of financially oriented statement(s), that indicates to the prospective customer, the measurable result they could experience by doing business with your organization? Well, don't worry if you might not be able to do that. It's a goal to strive toward.

This entire quest is about helping your prospects and current clients have an easier time finding the *truth* about your organization's offerings. Therefore, help them do that by being articulate and honest.

Success Number Three

The Organization This client is a major player in large-scale, customer retention and relationship management solutions. They develop relationship technology solutions and provide support for customers in several vertical industry sectors. The company is several billion in revenue.

The Premise/Problem/Challenge: One of their many sales offices was having a particular time raising the level of discussion within a specific, large target opportunity. The local account reps and sales manager had had numerous meetings and conversations with the Director of Marketing, and Director of Customer Relationship Management, over the course of about fourteen months. Things seemed to be going well, however management was beginning to wonder if the opportunity would ever come to fruition, or remain in the pipeline forever.

Every time the sales producers asked *ever so politely* for executive access/sponsorship, they were ushered right back down to the same levels they'd been dealing with over the last fourteen months. Upscale direct mail campaigns from corporate, and the offer of Superbowl tickets, had no affect on this company's willingness to grant our client access to their SVP of Marketing, SVP of Customer Relationship Management, and their EVP/CFO. However, the two lower-level individuals never missed an opportunity to be "lunched" by our client. There was definite frustration.

The Situation: The target opportunity was having an issue with customer retention. They'd spend "x" to attain the customer, only to learn "x" number of months later, that "x" number of customers would either stop their service, or move to another. This is a common challenge for companies in this industry, and significant enough to be on the radar screen of the senior executives. According to our client, the management of this company was dealing with this challenge as best they could. In this industry, they call this issue *churn*. Churn was costing this organization significant dollars, and the in-house CRM solution in place, wasn't addressing the problem very well.

The Consequence if Left Untouched: Clearly, our client needed executive sponsorship and couldn't get it. However, they worried about the potential negative repercussions of becoming more aggressive, or going over the heads of their two main contacts. If they did, they felt they'd lose all rapport, credibility, and perhaps the opportunity itself.

What about the opportunity? Our client sized it as a large-scale, data-warehousing solution, initially around five million in potential revenue, with the opportunity for additional growth from professional services, application consulting, etc. They were confident their offering was a more robust, industrial-strength solution, better capable of handling the prospect's needs, in comparison to the existing in-house solution in place.

However, by self admission, they had a hard time *articulating* or *quantifying* just how much their solution could impact the target company, bottom-line. The value proposition they had already put forth was *gray*. Secondly, timing was not the greatest. The target prospect had somehow communicated to our client that a major expenditure of hardware, software and support services probably would not fly, and that it certainly wasn't *top of mind* with senior management.

The two lower level contacts advised our client to; *"Just sit tight, and when the time is more appropriate, we'll bring it up again and see if we can get some mind share. You know that we like your solution, and we believe that we need it, but it's all about timing around here, at least for the kinds of dollars we're talking about if we move forward."*

As you can surmise, that message didn't find much *warmth* with our client's Regional Manager and Regional Vice President. They wanted the deal! This back and forth had been going on about *fourteen months*, not to mention the thousands of dollars invested in the selling and courting process. We were invited in to find a solution, build it, create the strategy, and then help implement it, to give them *the deal*. And this is basically what we did.

The Key Challenges: There were several:

1. When pushed, our client could not explain *by how much* their solution could benefit the target prospect in question, nor did they want to be *boxed into a corner* by committing themselves to a number.

2. Our client was having a hard time putting together the financial metrics, and the ROI story as to why this company should spend over five million dollars with them.

3. The *pitch* they had carried forward over the course of fourteen months was *soft* and difficult to quantify. It was packaged in these terms: *"Our solution will help you to lift this, reduce this, and improve that."* It needed some *hard-core calibration*, since we learned through additional research that the CEO of this organization had a net worth in excess of $250 million, and owned a significant percentage of the company's stock, even though they had been through several rounds of funding.

4. The incumbent solution our client was trying to displace wasn't exactly from a small, two-bit player. It was one of the largest software companies in the CRM space. Therefore, displacing them was going to be a challenge.

5. The client had an extensive reference list of customers who praised their solutions, many of which were several times larger than the target company they were trying to penetrate. However, this didn't seem to provide much of a lift, and it certainly didn't crash the doors down into their executive suites.

6. They were becoming nervous about being viewed as *too aggressive* and ruining any hope of attaining the business. In addition, the prospect had *no compelling event* where they disliked their current solution. Instead, the solution was doing an o.k. job, at least the lower level contacts thought so.

The Recommended Solution: We recommended the client do additional detailed research on the target prospect *and* the top ten senior officers. This provided the opportunity to learn more about the company's business, their industry, and the backgrounds of the top ten people, which provided insight into their personalities. This assisted us in more accurately *predicting* how they might respond to a more aggressive strategy.

Next, we worked as a team to dissect their current value proposition, taking the position as if we were the chairman of the board of the company we were trying to close. Clothed in that mentality and skeptical mindset, we then crafted a financially-oriented value proposition that would speak to five key executives we all agreed we needed access to:

- The President/CEO, who also happened to be the Chairman
- The Senior Vice President of Marketing
- The Vice President of Customer Relationship Management
- The Senior Vice President/Chief Financial Officer
- The Chief Operating Officer

These were the five executives we felt ought to pay attention to the new value proposition, if calibrated correctly. We also believed (based on the research), that nothing would happen unless these five people were *sold* on why they should move forward with the client solution. Based on our assessment of this company's chairman, the feeling was that *nobody moved* without his blessing. Therefore, the value proposition needed to speak to—and make common sense to him, or our client probably wouldn't get the business.

Next, the client's account team educated us on fourteen months of activity, so we were up to speed on all of the "back and forth". With that knowledge, we customized their value propositions even further, and wrote their *COL™ Template*—the actual letter that was sent in communicating the value proposition, their request for access, the agenda for how they would use their time if access was granted, and their desired/hoped for outcome. Why all of this in a letter? So that there were *no surprises* as to where they were trying to *drive* the prospect.

Their in-person presentation was then condensed and reordered from their standard *boiler-plate* PowerPoint presentation, which we shortened to ten minutes. We then taught them *how* to deliver the content in ten minutes, with a new style of presentation/delivery technique called *The 1/3rd...2/3rds*™. It is a specific pattern of presenting to a senior executive level audience, in five to ten minutes, usually without a laptop computer or projection system.

Lastly, the specific *COL*™ *launch strategy* was defined, designed to secure the audience they felt needed to hear their value proposition. In short, there was lots of preparation, however the size of the opportunity warranted it.

The Revised Approach: The new value proposition turned out well. The client was pleased with its clarity, especially for those they needed to engage:

"If you do business with our organization—more specifically—if you install our large-scale data warehousing and CRM solution, we can find you approximately eighteen million dollars in new revenues over a three year time frame, via our customer relationship management and retention solutions.

Even more specifically—we feel confident that we can:

1. *Dramatically reduce the number of customers who leave your company after you've worked so hard to acquire them—and improve your customer retention rate to the tune of...*

2. *Finding/retaining approximately twenty-three million in new revenues over a three year period—with an investment of approximately five million dollars over that same time frame; netting you approximately eighteen million in new money.*

After doing our homework on your organization and your CRM operation, and after some preliminary financial modeling; this is our value proposition to you and your organization, and why we are formally requesting senior level access. This is the "net-net" of how we believe we can financially impact your organization, and address a few of the specific goals you state in your most recent annual report."

Remember, even though their value proposition was clear, they still needed the *access*. Therefore, by using The COL™, they broadcasted their value proposition in a manner that would hopefully provide permission to present and elaborate, face-to-face.

That being said, we custom wrote their four page *COL™ letter*, and selected nine senior executives inside the organization who would receive it *simultaneously*.

The Result: It worked. Our client was granted access to the levels desired without any pushback. In fact, there were several senior executives present. —Guess who else showed up? The Chairman/CEO— long enough to hear the core message, which we assumed he had already read in his personalized copy of *The COL™ letter*.

As a result, our client had a highly engaged and positive exchange, which led to permission and senior executive sponsorship to refine the financial model, based on additional information the prospect provided. This was followed by high-level technology-oriented meetings to verify that the solution would properly "marry into" existing platforms and architectures. The rest was history. Our client was pleased.

For those wondering if our client damaged their rapport with the two lower level contacts, it was quite the opposite. How much time do you think these two individuals get to spend with their chairman? They ended up *thanking our client* for the *new-found positive exposure to their own senior management*; exposure they couldn't seem to garner on their own.

Success Number Four

The Organization: A publicly-held international manufacturer, marketer and provider of hand-held wireless email messaging products and services. The company's revenues when we began working with them were approximately $100 million, and we were told their market cap was in excess of $1 billion.

The Premise/Problem/Challenge: The client was not experiencing any significant problems per say. Things were bustling along rather well, however management felt they could do even better if they could get higher up inside large, potential users of their products. They could then drive home the core benefits of their versatile devices. At the time, they were targeting organizations that might need 500 to 1,000 or more of their devices.

The client was also a Microsoft Partner, one of several hundred Microsoft Certified Solution Providers—an MCSP for short. They had heard me speak at two Microsoft World Fusion Annual Conventions.

The Situation: In addition to wanting higher levels of access and exposure to close more lucrative deals, they were also looking for options on how to expand their revenue from their channel organization, with client partners and value added reseller companies. The client was (and still is) on a "roll", but they wanted to meet or exceed all forecasts, and be smart about how they were going to market.

The Consequence if Left Untouched: The client had a feeling that a few of their competitors, which were major telecommunications companies, could give them serious pain at any time. Hence management was on their toes. Speed to market was critical, as was the ability to raise the awareness level of what their devices could really do, so they could close larger deals. Furthermore, one could argue that their products were a "nice to have"—not a "need to have".

The Recommended Solution: Their existing value proposition was hard to quantify, even though they manufactured a great-looking device that served a definite need, and worked quite well. They also had an impressive customer list.

We worked with senior management challenging them on the audiences to whom they were currently selling—basically mid to lower levels inside the information technology departments of large organizations. Perhaps this was one of the reasons the sales cycles were longer than they wanted them to be.

As we came to agreement on changing the target audience they wanted to attract, they educated us on their typical sales process, so we could understand where deals would "fall off", stall, or *go silent*. We also wanted to understand from their perspective, the levels of individuals within prospect organizations, who would *involve themselves* in the decision process, based on certain levels of expenditures.

After learning these elements, we created a new *front-end— a sales process* in actuality, that better qualified potential opportunities, earlier in the process. At the same time this new front-end eliminated several meetings from their process. How? By crafting a value proposition that appealed to key senior level executives linking hard number productivity increases that could be substantiated, to the device. This allowed their prospects to perform a rough calculation on the financial benefits the device would provide based on their employee size, and respective salaries—all before determining if they were going to grant our client access.

The Circle of Leverage® System was also an integral part of the solution, since an articulate value proposition by itself, doesn't automatically cause the normal barriers of entry to come crashing down. Therefore, we taught them *The COL™* and custom wrote their *COL® Templates* and value propositions to achieve their objectives.

The New Approach: *"We are requesting a 30 minute in-person presentation—to present a 15 minute condensed capabilities overview, and a quick, on-the-spot financial ROI analysis of how we can—through our product—find an extra 30-60 minutes of additional time for each one of your sales and field support professionals per day; which will allow you to increase the productivity levels of these individuals in the range of 5% on the low side—by up to 15% on the high side—throughout your entire enterprise.*

This is our value proposition to you and your organization."

The Result: We have heard that their market cap was recently north of two billion dollars.

TEETH—the financial metrics inside your core message(s), can without question, help your organization close more business. However, as we've mentioned, do not be disappointed if your product, service or solution offerings don't lend themselves to being metriced. Perhaps it is difficult to secure the data from clients that would allow your company to build a financially-oriented value proposition.

Some clients are unable to use financially-oriented metrics, yet their refined value propositions did help accomplish their goals. Therefore, our coaching is to get as "tight" as you possibly can with your messages.

Measurable ROI Anyone?

As evidenced by the client case histories, this subject matter is worth your organization's time because the correct value propositions can provide immense payback in several ways.

They can help motivate and empower your organization's field producers more than any one-day motivational seminar, since the benefits of those are usually short-lived.

A clear and focused value proposition can *endure*, and provide a *rallying point* for your employees. It can also help crystallize in everyone's mind: *"Yes—that is how we benefit other organizations."*

Good value propositions actually create *passion* and *focus* around your organization's charter, because they help your people *see* more clearly, how they are benefiting others. Furthermore, they can help *drive revenues, reduce closing cycles, reduce cost of sales, and improve margins*. These benefits are core to every organization.

We continue to help clients *find the truth* about what their offerings really bring to another customer, in regards to *true financial value*—in our efforts to extend the business relationships our clients have worked very hard to attain.

CHAPTER ELEVEN
You're Too Slow—and You Take Too Long to Get to the Point

Most clients want their sales and business development professionals to achieve higher levels of access and exposure, earlier on in their selling process. Our programs help deliver those results.

As we ask our clients about the specific levels of access they desire more exposure to, we also inquire about the nature of their *boiler-plate* presentation(s)—the *dog and pony* shows they give, once they're in. Here's how clients typically respond.

Nine times out of ten they will say something like this: *"We weren't planning to discuss the presentation of our message with your company. We've got that nailed. We don't have any trouble with that. That's not why we've come to you. Plus, we've already got a presentation skills vendor that assists us with the content and delivery. And to be honest, it's not that difficult. Our sales people all carry laptop computers, so they just pull them out and blast through their boiler-plate PowerPoint presentation, which we obviously customize as need be, based on our audience. It works really slick. So again—let's just focus on the access piece, and our message, o.k.?"*

This is a great place for us to ask a few more questions:

Q1: Do you feel that most organization's boiler-plate PowerPoint presentations are too short, or *too long*?

Q2: Do you feel that most organization's boiler-plate presentations are *too detailed* with information the prospect or client might say they don't really need to know, or are they just right?

Q3: Are most organization's PowerPoint presentations calibrated to *mid-level management* and *below*, or to a senior level audience?

Q4: Guess who typically does not like sitting through PowerPoint oriented—laptop projected presentations: mid-level management or *senior level executives*?

Q5: Whom do you think has a shorter, more "ornery" attention span: mid-level management or *senior level executives*?

Based on the most popular answers which are *italicized*, are you beginning to see why it is common to hear a senior executive say (right during your presentation): *"Do I need to be here for this? Perhaps my people need to hear this more than I do. Perhaps it's premature for me to be involved at this point."*

The *facts* suggest that in reality, most organizations and producers have *so much information* packed into their boiler-plate presentations that they are a *turn-off* for the recipient to sit through—so much so, that sometimes the audiences you've worked so hard to get in front of, actually leave, or *dial out* before you finish.

Re-Torque the Way You Deliver
Your Value Propositions

The logical progression of an articulate value proposition containing *TEETH,* combined with The COL™ System to gain more frequent senior levels of exposure, creates an interesting dynamic for clients. These elements challenge the client to condense the way in which they deliver their in-person presentations, because often, they have more of the correct audiences they desire in front of them, earlier on in their selling cycle. This creates a dilemma for the client—what does the audience really need to hear?

We work with clients in this area as well. Usually, it involves reformatting and condensing the content of their existing presentation, to be *calibrated* to the levels of executives they will have in front of them. We have also helped re-torque the *method* and *manner* in which they present—*much* shorter, snappier, and to-the-point, which senior executives love.

Our suggestion: Go through your organization's standard boilerplate presentation and weed out the "unnecessaries and nice-to-knows." Then have your people present it back to you, while you play "senior exec." Be tough on each other. Drill down to the core nuggets of what really *needs* to be in your initial presentation, because when it's "real-world" time, this is exactly how prospects and clients will be with you and your producers.

Deliver with Maximum Moxy in 5 to 10 Minutes Max

Many of us talk too much in business meetings, so talk less. Focus your energy on a core presentation that can be delivered in five to ten minutes max. First of all, it can be done. Secondly, your clients will love this new format.

We have created a methodology and delivery technique for condensing, and then delivering your core message and value propositions in about 10 minutes max—*to a senior executive audience—without a laptop or projection system.*

This delivery technique is *very effective* and *pays large dividends* for those senior executives and sales producers trained on this skill-set. The recipients of this style of presentation usually can't say enough about it. If you're interested in learning more, contact us.

It All Works Together

Your message and value propositions—access at the right levels—the people presenting your value propositions—and the presentation itself. These are a few of the components that make up the *front-end* of your organization's selling process. You could argue that they also encompass the marketing or go-to-market strategy of an organization.

It doesn't really matter what type of sales process or sales training programs you use within your organization, because if they don't properly address the above components, how much do you really have?

CHAPTER TWELVE
You're Not Fixed Yet

Based on our observations and experience, a significant percentage of senior executives view the training industry in such a light, where you go to a training program, and then boom—*you're "fixed"*.

There doesn't seem to be much *tolerance* for learning. Many want it to be like a *fast food* experience. You're in, and then you're out. You've taken the course, gleaned what you felt was valuable, and now *voila—you're fixed*. Not to mention of course, that the *implementation* and *execution* of what was *just* learned will be flawless the first time out of the gate. In reality, this is rarely ever the case regardless of the program's content. However, the perception and the desire to *cookie-cutter* the learning process persists, and has for years. Maybe it will never change.

When people go to a weight loss clinic to lose weight, learn how to eat right and exercise more, what percentage actually succeeds the first time? It's probably pretty low, wouldn't you think, as evidenced by the fact that the weight loss industry is several billion dollars in revenue—*every year*.

For those who golf, let's take golf lessons as an example. Have you ever hired a golf professional to teach you a few new pointers? — Maybe an adjustment to your swing, follow-through, your stance, or the way in which you hold the club. If you have, you probably did what you were taught—*for a while*—but only until it didn't give you the *immediate* results you wanted. Then you probably put aside much of what you were taught. Want proof? Look at the size of the golf lesson industry.

What if Tiger Woods, one of *the* most accomplished golfers in history, took the time to personally show you his secrets about how to hold the club, how to stand, and how to properly follow-through?

Most people would probably attempt to do everything he showed you, *unless it felt weird,* or didn't produce the results as fast as you thought you should have them. And if this were to happen, some might even discount the things the great Tiger Woods taught them.

Can you hear those who might say: *"You know, Tiger personally showed me a new way to hold the club, but you know—it just didn't feel right to me. So I've gone back to what feels more comfortable— at least for me."*

All of us have a small amount of fickleness to our personalities. Therefore, just because you've gone through a course and become enlightened on some new thing, or in this case you've read this book and now feel you're *fixed*, may we give you one small reminder:

This is Serious Stuff. Please Treat It That Way

I have attempted to present the content in this book to guide you and your organization in helping create, condense, refine, or recalibrate your messages and value propositions, so you experience even more success going forward.

With that said, **your level of success as an organization is directly connected to your people's ability to articulate the answers to:** *"Why you, and exactly how can you help benefit us?"*

Therefore, this *is* very serious stuff, and we encourage you to treat it that way. This ability and skill-set are critical to your continued success in business. If you would like to discuss additional assistance, we invite you to contact us at **www.strategic–access.com,** or by phone at 952-447-5246.

Practice a Few Hundred Times.
Learn to Hit It Correctly

As mentioned earlier, *rarely does anyone nail anything the first time.*

Your new value propositions need to be tested on your target audiences for you to receive legitimate feedback. This feedback will help you sharpen your value propositions, until you *cut your way through the clutter—to your desired audiences— so that you have your "day-in-the-sun", and can present your value propositions to those who have the power to give you what you want.*

Therefore, listen for the feedback, and tweak accordingly until you *hit it correctly.*

Whom do you think practices more than Tiger Woods? Probably no one. Look what he's been able to accomplish. You too can improve your levels of success by taking this content seriously—and *practicing a few hundred times, until you nail it.*

Remember the *principles* that are the *bedrock* of the material we have just covered:

Respectfulness—honesty—fairness—stewardship—simple courteousness—directness—becoming more worthy—and excellent ethics.

Use the methodology and field-proven framework herein to help your prospects and clients *find the truth* about your organization's offerings, and we will become more valuable to each others' endeavors.

Use this material and come back to it frequently. Give the book to a friend, business acquaintance, or maybe even a business partner— so *they* improve the way in which they do business with you. That way, everyone wins.

Thank you again. I hope you feel this material was worth your time and investment.

— Wishing you continued success.

The very best,
Michael A. Boylan

AN EXECUTIVE OVERVIEW
STRATEGIC ACCESS™
A BOYLAN GROUP, INC. COMPANY

Strategic Access™ is a respected thought leader in *enterprise revenue acceleration, compression of sales & closing cycles, selling expense reduction,* and *margin improvement,* working with the senior management, sales and business development organizations of Fortune 2000 companies.

In the technology sector, clients include Microsoft, LogicaCMG, CapGemini Ernst & Young, ADP, Ceridian, NEC, NCR, Keane, Administaff, Mitel Networks, Norstan, PLATO Learning, and Research In Motion, Ltd., (maker of the Blackberry).

The company is an international provider of strategic consulting, assessment, executive workshops, training programs and outsourced managed services, focused around teaching, coaching, and helping implement field-proven "best practice" business processes and repeatable methodologies, that effectively help the sales and business development organizations & senior management:

—Accelerate revenues, impacting top-line revenue

—Compress closing cycles by 20% to 50%

—Reduce cost of sales levels by up to 1/3rd

—Enhancing margins

A NEW STANDARD

Based on a track record of client acceptance and **seamless integration with existing sales processes** — our proprietary methodologies are creating the new standard used by accomplished sales organizations interested in gaining access and more exposure to senior executive level decision makers faster, more frequently, and earlier on in the selling process — in their efforts to drive more closed business in a top-down fashion.

Our programs are based on specific skill sets around **repeatable, step-by-step methodologies providing measurable positive impact.** They are tailored for sales and business development professionals and senior client account managers responsible for **growing the revenue streams from their existing customer accounts**—meaning—they already have access inside the account with multiple contacts, but wish to expand their exposure, influence, and/or executive levels of access, to provide progress updates, new solution offerings, etc.

They are also tailored for professionals charged with **finding new business,** in a **true prospecting or "hunter" type mode** within targeted prospect opportunities that clients have identified as potentially lucrative.

Clients range in revenues between $50 million to several billion and have between 50 to 500 or more sales professionals. We work with an organization's senior leadership in the parent company, and/or respective business units — and their sales and business development organizations. Clients may also involve their sales support and marketing organizations, accelerating consistency and cohesion of the methodologies throughout the organization — maximizing return on investment.

We serve clients in the technology sector, with a view toward expanding into manufacturing, insurance, banking, financial services, healthcare, and other industry sectors.

POSITION IN THE MARKETPLACE

We provide higher levels of *access* for our clients, *faster, more frequently,* and *earlier on in their selling process.* Therefore, we do not view ourselves in the sales training business.

Most clients have a sales process in place, which our proprietary methodologies *front-end*, in a seamless, *"bolt-on"* fashion, further enhancing their existing sales process.

Strategic Access works with the senior leadership of business units, and their respective sales and business development organizations, helping to further *crystallize, condense,* and *calibrate their existing value propositions* around the business unit's product/service/solution offerings, so they have more *TEETH*—providing more traction at the "CXO" level.

We then train and help implement repeatable, best-practice methodologies that assist in gaining access to the desired senior executive decision makers, faster, more frequently, and earlier in their sales process.

These methodologies can also be *tactically calibrated* and executed, through our **SPECIAL OPS STRIKE FORCE MANAGED SERVICES** offering, to assist clients in closing complex, large-scale "RFP" type opportunities already in progress—as well as on deals that may have been awarded to another provider, but have not yet been signed.

FINANCIAL VALUE PROPOSITION

Clients who consistently implement and apply these field-proven, best practice methodologies throughout their sales and business development organizations are able to:

—Compress sales & closing cycles in their business units by 20% - 50%

—Reduce cost of sales levels by up to 1/3rd, which typically frees up millions in cash flow

—Accelerate revenue, enhance margins, sometimes growing top-line revenue

KEYNOTE SPEAKING

The founder of Strategic Access and creator of it's methodologies has delivered **general session keynote addresses** for some of the most respected companies in America, for company-wide annual sales meetings, quarterly events and regional meetings. As one of the **highest rated general session keynote speakers at the Microsoft World Fusion Annual Conventions,** and **the highest rated general session keynote speaker of all time** by the **Advertising Specialties Institute Annual Conventions,** Michael is a proven and seasoned professional.

For information on keynote fees and availability, please call 952-447-5246, or email us at info@strategic–access.com. A conference call can be scheduled to learn the objectives of your event. We can then provide several options for your consideration.

HOW CAN WE ASSIST YOUR BUSINESS— ARE WE A GOOD FIT?

In our efforts to be efficient and a good steward of your time, we have a simple process that takes approximately 30 – 60 minutes, helping determine if there is a potential fit.

The confidential **Mutual Pre-Qualification Process, helps both parties rapidly pre-qualify each other, saving time and money.**

The process works by visiting our website at **www.strategic–access.com** — and clicking on ARE WE A GOOD FIT?

A short list of questions are provided for you to answer and provide your prospective, which, once submitted to us, allows for a mutually productive discussion — to help both organizations quickly determine what the potential benefits would be! You will be pleased with the company's level of detail, and commitment to service.

Thank you. We look forward to hearing from you.

Contact Information

For more information, and for
a complete listing of the company's
offerings, we invite you to visit
our Website at:

www.strategic–access.com

You may also write, fax,
call or email us at:

Strategic Access™
9941 Deerbrook Drive, Suite 200
Chanhassen, Minnesota 55317
Phone (952) 447-5246
Fax (952) 447-5247

Email: info@strategic–access.com

We welcome your emails on
how this material is benefitting
your organization. Send us your
experiences and success stories.

We look forward to hearing from you!